# THE WISDOM OF AFRICAN MYTHOLOGY

## by John J. Ollivier

**TOP OF THE MOUNTAIN PUBLISHING**
Largo, Florida 34643-5117 U.S.A.

**TOP OF THE MOUNTAIN PUBLISHING**
11701 South Belcher Road, Suite 123
Largo, Florida 34643-5117 U.S.A.
SAN 287-590X
FAX (24 hour) (813) 536-3681
PHONE (813) 530-0110

Copyright 1994 by John J. Ollivier

*Library of Congress Cataloging in Publication Data*
Ollivier, John J.
Wisdom of African Mythology / by John J. Ollivier.
p. cm.
ISBN 1-56087-023-0: $14.95
1. Folklore—Africa. 2. Mythology, African. 3. Proverbs, African. 4. Legends—Africa. I. Title.
GR350.046  1994
398'.096—dc20                    91-35050 CIP

Cover Design: Dr. Tag Powell
Manufactured in the United States

# A TRIBUTE TO NEGRITUDE

For beauty is Black
and wisdom is Black
for endurance is Black
and courage is Black
for patience is Black
and irony Black
for charm is Black
and magic Black
for love is Black
and hip swinging Black
for dance is Black
and rhythm Black
for art is Black
and movement Black
for laughter is Black
for joy is Black
for peace is Black
for life is Black

An African poet

# TABLE OF CONTENTS

# Table of Contents

# FOREWORD

*The Wisdom of African Mythology* is much needed... to educate ourselves, our children, our public on the importance of multiculturalism. As an educator, I can attest to the growing importance of having a complete and intelligent understanding of one's own culture, as well as the cultures and heritages of other people.

We can easily see in our current social scene that history is beginning to repeat itself...rioting, racially motivated verbal attacks and physical brutality. These actions are not those of a healthy world, nor are they of a satisfied people.

That's where *The Wisdom of African Mythology* can help to play a powerful and critical educational role. It teaches the reader in a simplified, fun way about African folktales, mythology and beliefs. This book presents culture in a positive manner. It explains, it details, and it doesn't discriminate against any particular culture. Best of all, it's easy-to-understand.

The KEY to multicultural education is teaching neutrality with emphasis on EVERY type of culture and background. Therefore, not only is African history important—so is Caucasian, Asian,

Native American and Hispanic. John J. Ollivier is headed in the right direction... bringing the African culture to light so that it will appeal to all colors, all ages, all people.

I recommend this book to be read by anyone who is willing to increase their awareness while enjoying a scholarly examination of Africa's heritage. This book is for the reader who is willing to open his or her mind and heart towards universal understanding, and take a sense of pride in knowing the roots of a fundamental culture—the African culture.

*The Wisdom of African Mythology* would be a great teaching tool to use in multicultural education. It is simplified enough to appeal to elementary and grade school children...to read at storytime hours. It is also ideal for the high school or university level classroom because of its educational value without the boredom of textbook language and format.

I will definitely put it to good use in my multicultural lectures and courses across the country. Why? It's appealing... the wit, the humor and (of course) the mythology found within this book will go a long way for audiences because stories are easier to remember. After all, we did grow up hearing, at least, one folktale that had an indelible impression about humanity on our minds and values!

Much praise is given to Mr. Ollivier's writing efforts, his social concerns, and his dedication to accuracy! I strongly encourage you to read this book. It's your small step towards exercising your understanding of how we, as a global nation, can build a gentlier and kinder world...where cultural and ethnic diversity is seen as a strength, not a weakness...and moreso, as an enlightened humanity!

Patrick C. Coggins, Ph.D., J.D.
Jessie Ball duPont Chair
Professor of Education
Stetson University, Deland, Florida

# AUTHOR'S NOTE

I think it's hard to put in words
    Traditions of the blacks.
Yet this is what I'll try to do
    By keeping to the facts.

I'll write of their ancestral faith,
    Of origins and death,
Of whence man came and where man goes
    When breathing final breath.

I'll speak of black men's ancient gods
    And how things came to be,
And who it was that set aside
    The dry land from the sea.

I'll speak about the sun and moon
    And why the rainbow's ray,
And why the bat flies through the night
    And why it sleeps all day.

The stories of their animals
    Will entertain us all.
Their fables have such wit and charm
    That readers are enthralled.

We'll learn the values black men held
    Within their family life.
We'll learn their pride of heritage
    Which has withstood such strife.

We'll see them seek causality,
    Like wise men always do,
Who know there must be reasons for
    The goals that gods pursue.

So listen to these stories now,
    And in black wisdom bask.
They'll entertain and educate,
    And what more could one ask.

# INTRODUCTION

To discuss the mythology of a continent as large as Africa is not an easy task. There were a myriad of unwritten languages spread throughout a multitude of peoples in a vast area of land. In spite of many diversities, there was a certain uniformity to Africa, in the regions south of the Sahara, omitting the Islamized cultures to the north. Africa possessed this uniformity in spite of the many outside forces that influenced its history.

The world's most far reaching movements found their greatest progress on African soil. It was through Africa that Christianity moved to become the religion of the world; it was through Africa that Islam spread its crescent of conquest and convert as it moved into western Europe. Much later Africa was exploited and plundered by Europeans in a manner contemptible beyond belief. Rape, torture and murder marked the paths of these Europeans as they marauded their way through the "dark continent." They destroyed natural boundaries, and split cultures bound together by ties of language and religion.

Perhaps the Europeans' greatest cruelty to Africans was the selling of slaves. Between 1500 and 1810, eleven to fifteen million human beings were captured in Africa and sold into slavery. Families were divided. Children were sold apart from parents. Husbands and wives were separated. No tie of blood or family was respected as loved ones were torn apart and shipped like cattle to Europe's American colonies to serve as laborers. Sixteen percent of those slaves died on overcrowded ships from starvation or disease during the six week trip to America. This journey was called the Middle Passage. Often times the dead and the living were found chained together in the heat of the ship's hold. One can readily understand the sarcasm of one black to another when accused of cruelty: "Do you think I'm a white man?"

When Africa was no longer plundered by traders and merchants, it was then exploited by Imperialism: Europeans robbed her of her riches and natural resources under the name of Colonialism, whose most degrading evil was to strip Africa of the responsibility of conducting its own affairs and to convince the world Africans were little more than savages. This subjugation built an inferiority complex in many Africans from which they have ever since sought to emerge. A movement known as Negritude, developed by African poets and scholars in this century, has sought to remove this complex by proudly expressing authentic African values and culture with which Africans everywhere can identify.

Is it too much to ask, that in the future, Africa writes its own history? Is it unreasonable Africans would seek dignity, honor and independence? Surely, Africans prefer self-government with risks to servitude with tranquility. The right of a people to determine its own destiny is not a matter of color. It's a matter of inalienable rights. Africa had a glorious past which long predated those ugly centuries where she became exploited. Today, Africa can create, out of that glorious past, an equally glorious future. Centuries ago, Africa possessed universities and cities, art and culture, and a civilization equivalent to anything known to Europe of that day. She had kings and rulers before which the royalty of Europe bowed in admiration; she had castles and courts before which they stood in awe.

Africans excelled in human relations. It is in this capacity they can be an example to the rest of the world today. For Africans, life has always meant the pursuit of happiness rather than seeking some abstract beauty or truth. They found that happiness in the communal life of the family. Universal love must precede universal peace. The root of this universal love is family love, and unless it is rooted, it will not grow. Africans can teach the world that universal peace ultimately rests on the cultivation of family love. Africans can teach the world that love must begin in the home.

Communal activity was an essential part of African life. We see this in their games and dances. Even hunting and fishing were done in groups, as were planting and harvesting. This communal gathering was not due to some physical necessity, but to a genuine love of others. Africans are noted for a strong sense of humor and a disdain for melancholy. This characteristic precludes the possibility of discouragement or dejection, although their history is one of abuse and constant mistreatment at the hands of others. But in spite of past sufferings, Africans will always make molehills out of pain and mountains out of those things that bring joy. They are a happy, forgiving people. These are the gifts Africans must give to a world which stands in such need of them. As someone once said: "If

Africans were disposed to seek revenge on those who abused them, their history would have been completely different."

Because of the African's predisposition toward communal happiness and forgiveness, Africans can waste love on foreigners who are ungrateful in return. They can raise a white man's child with love, knowing they will receive only criticism in return. They can refuse to be rich, if the cost is being cruel. They can know white men think God created blacks to be of service to those He created white, yet still not hold a grudge. Africans realize all of these possibilities and still they forgive — not because they are fools, but because they are innately kind.

Moreover, Africans dislike imposing themselves on others. It is not because they have nothing to say or nothing to be proud of, but because they think it rude to act otherwise. Colonialism knew nothing of the African's soul. That is why it failed. What we seek to portray in this little work is the African who was and the African who still is. He or she is the same. May the reader come to meet this indivdual as the "real" African!

# AFRICAN FOLKTALES

All nations have memories. In the past, most nations also had a class of professional minstrels, bards and storytellers who recollected and retold the nation's history so future generations would know their country's former glories. Myths are a kind of sacred history of how things came to be and these tales of past heroes provided young children with models of behavior to imitate. These ancient myths might seem trivial to us today, but in ages past, every nation's myths were extremely important as a primitive but intellectual efforts to understand the phenomena which influenced their daily lives.

There is no art more ancient than the art of story telling. This was especially true in ancient Africa where oral narrative was usually accompanied by music and dance. Africans loved the oral tale. They had no written language, isolated as they were from literate people by desserts, forests and seas. Perhaps that's why they so excelled in storytelling. Although most stories were told to entertain simple folks around a camp fire, those same stories give scholars today a clear insight into the customs and beliefs of primitive minds from days-of-old.

Ancient folktales demonstrate a common psychic unity between present and ancient peoples. The same emotions which were in them are in us. Some emotions are common to humanity itself: grief at death, joy at birth, love of parents for children, and jealousy among lovers. There is hate and fear in every man's life. African folktales originated when men, animals and trees were considered very much alike. Trees and animals were depicted as people. Animals spoke like men, and there was a common friendship between them. The basis of myth is not thought, but feelings which trace a picture of the society from which the myth arose. A nation's lore reflects its social reality. Folktales were handed down from one generation to the next. Everyone who told them accepted them as truth. They served as an explanation for the accepted conduct in people's lives showing the way society acted from time immemorial.

African folktales probably had a collective authorship, and were added to as they were told and retold by the "griot," the storyteller, to amuse and entertain. No matter how varied the tale might be, there was always a common element, the introduction: "A long, long time ago, even before our ancestors knew the use of fire, when they ate grass like the animals..." These folktales were told even before the difference between men and animals was clearly recognized by Africans.

Folktales were oral narratives explaining their tribal history, values and rituals to preserve them for posterity. Myths came from rituals, not rituals from myths. Their stories expressed a tribal wisdom and were marked by a naive morality. They rendered, with their characteristic simplicity, the primitive impressions of natural and supernatural forces which influenced their lives. They often mixed fact with fancy, for so much was beyond their powers of understanding. Perhaps these oral stories have lost something of their power and mystery by the written word. This loss can be expected, especially since the storyteller or "griot" added so much to the story by his artistry, gestures, voice and expressions.

The ancient Africans were instinctively superstitious. What is now considered natural and nor-

mal, they considered supernatural. There was no
other explanation for lightning and thunder, or
unusual natural phenomena. Their folktales were
a kind of degraded mythology to explain excep-
tional events. The past and present coexisted happily in African  mythology. Storytellers made no
reference to time. Tales were set among indefinite
periods of mythological time, as "In olden days" or
"Once upon a time." In this mythological time
frame, figures were either human or non-human,
or perhaps a combination of both.

Tribal concerns were often depicted in tales
which portrayed animal characters. We need not
interpret these tales. They interpret themselves. Although the stories included every kind of animal,
the spider was the great hero of African folktales.
He was the king of cunning who overcame every
sort of intrigue. He was the legendary hero that
easily conquered every obstacle villagers set before
him. Many scholars of mythology claim that the
people of ancient Africa considered the spider the
power of the sun personified.

# ANANSEE THE SPIDER

The fables of dark Africa,
    Not known to the outsider,
Made heroes of their animals,
    Especially, the spider.

The spider's name was Anansee,
    Most clever, but quite cross.
He had but one desire in life,
    To be the whole world's boss.

He stole the wisdom of the world,
    In spider knavery.
So no one else could share it,
    He hid it up a tree.

He put this wisdom in a bag,
    And tied it round his waist.
He then set out to climb the tree,
    Proceeding with great haste.

He hung the bag in front of him,
    Which made the climbing tough.
His hands could hardly reach the tree,
    So as he climbed he puffed.

His son below began to laugh,
    And mock his father's sense.
For if he were so worldly wise,
    Why did he act so dense?

"You should have put the bag in back."
    The son called to his father.
"And then as you would climb the tree,
    It wouldn't be a bother."

The angry spider in his pride,
    Then hurled the bag to earth.
He aimed it at his scoffing son,
    To counteract his mirth.

The bag was broken by the fall.
    Its contents strewn around.
And wisdom scattered everywhere,
    As bag crashed to the ground.

The tribesmen rushed from woods and plains,
    To grab the scattered treasure.
And each man got a little bit,
    But each man got his measure.

# Anansee the Spider

The spider acted foolishly,
    So had to share his prize.
The spider's loss was mankind's gain,
    For now each man is wise.

The spider wished what wisdom gave,
    He wanted to be free.
But greed held Anansee enslaved,
    And left him up a tree.

Yes, greed enslaves and then destroys,
    As greed is wont to do.
And so unless you fight its lure,
    It'll do the same to you.

Greed will corrupt and then consume
    Most everything it touches.
And like the spider, it destroys
    Whatever's in its clutches.

There's wisdom in this ancient myth,
    Black Africa has taught us.
We're wiser than the spider was,
    Unless his greed has caught us.

That's why the blacks are generous
    With the little they possess.
They picked up what Anansee dropped,
    'Twas wisdom's righteousness.

Anansee's son deserves our praise,
    And possibly a hug.
Except for him, we each would be
    Less wise than some dumb bug.

*Kita pendant enclosing*
*holy verses from Mauritania*

# THE SYMBOL OF ETERNITY

Men have always been fascinated by snakes. They crawl without feet. They are mysterious. They are feared as dangerous to all living things. The snake is regarded by some as immortal because it sheds its skin and still continues to live. Art depicts the snake as a symbol of eternity with its tail held in its mouth like a circle that has no beginning nor end.

The python is the favorite snake in African mythology. It was often deified. When god created the earth, the snake carried him about in its mouth. Each night when they stopped, the snake's excrement made great mountains. When man dug into them, he discovered many treasures. The mountains became so numerous the creator feared the earth would sink into the sea from their weight. He asked the snake to coil itself around the earth to support it. If it loosed its coils the earth would disintegrate. The snake lived in the sea because it hated heat. When the snake shifted its weight earthquakes occurred.

God commissioned monkeys to feed the snake. If they failed to do so, the snake would eat its own tail which supported the earth and the earth would fall into the sea. That would be the end of the world. There are many myths dealing with snakes among various African tribes. In the following rhyme, I seek to depict a myth of the Kono tribe of Sierra Leone about the snake and the origin of death.

# THE ORIGIN OF DEATH

The chief god made both man and wife,
    And then sent them a son.
He told them they would never lose.
    The endless life he'd spun.

When they'd grow old he said he'd send,
    New skins for their old frame.
He promised this and kept his word,
    And sent skins when time came.

He placed new skins into a bag,
    And gave it to a dog.
"Please take these skins to my dear friends,
    Who've kept my Decalogue."

The dog met other animals,
    As he traversed the jungle.
He joined with them in partying,
    As god's plan he'd soon bungle.

They asked him what was in the bag.
    He told them of God's plan.
A snake who overheard him speak,
    Had other plans for man.

The snake then stole the fresh new skins,
    And slithered off with speed.
He shared these skins with other snakes,
    Who gained from his misdeed.

So now it's snakes who change their skins,
    As man was meant to do.
Recall this fact the next time that
    You see snakes in a zoo.

The dog reported sheepishly,
    To man what had occurred.
And man reported then to God,
    The details that he'd heard.

It was too late; God's die was cast,
    So man and wife both cried,
For reasons all have since known well,
    For since then man has died.

So is it any wonder then,
    That snakes are so despised.
They undermined the plans of God,
    And so should be chastised.

For what they do in shedding skins,
    Revitalizing life,
Was meant in God's plan to be done
    By man and by man's wife.

And what about the lousy dog,
    That claims he's man's best friend.
If he had been responsible,
    Our lives would never end.

# THE ROLE OF WOMEN IN
## AFRICAN LIFE

To understand the role of women in African life we must understand the view Africans had of the world as composed of forces which ceaselessly interacted. To the African everything was force. There was no division between the animate and the inanimate. Some forces were simply greater than others. Lesser forces like water provided service to man who was a greater force. To have force was the essence of being to the African. To exist was to possess force.

The highest force was God. He was a force who created himself. God was the center from which all other forces flowed. He was the vital force which caused all of creation. After God came primordial ancestors. They were almost divine. They interceded with God for man. They deeply influenced harvests, epidemics and every phase of human life. Next in the order of forces came the more recent dead. They were also intercessors. The dead of any particular clan were worshipped by that clan.

There was a hierarchy of forces in the world. The only difference between a man and a rock was the degree of force each possessed. Since a woman was the source and guardian of the life force, she played a primary role in African life and was loved, honored and respected. She was the guarantor of the clan's future. In many tribes nobility and family inheritance were transmitted through the mother. Women, and especially mothers, played a prominent role in every phase of African life. The African woman today needs not be liberated. She has been free for thousands of years.

# AFRICAN WOMEN

The women of dark Africa,
    Truly treasured life.
And so they found fulfillment in,
    Being someone's wife.

For "wifing" led to motherhood,
    And motherhood to birth,
Which was the greatest glory which
    A woman gave to earth.

For in that birth all life lived on
    From distant ages past.
Ancestors in their offspring lived
    As long as love would last.

Parents lived in children's lives,
    Yes, even after death,
Remembrance in a family's love
    Served as some kind of breath.

I'm sure that women "libbers," though,
    Would think this neolithic,
And pity the poor Hottentots,
    Who think their kids terrific.

The "libbers" simple cannot see
    What feminism is.
All life for them is quite confused,
    A complicated quiz.

They do not know what freedom means,
    Or that it has a price.
And what they wish, they think must be,
    Without a sacrifice.

A woman's life can't be a wish.
    A statement it must be.
Made not by voice, but by her life,
    Or else she can't be free.

For freedom's not its own reward,
    As feminists might say.
It's but a means; it's not an end.
    And means are made of clay.

It's but a means to happiness,
    Worth any sacrifice.
All means are cheap for priceless goals,
    Yes, cheap at twice the price.

So freedom "from" means freedom "for,"
    If not, the word's bizarre.
Unless there is finality,
    One's reach has reached too far.

Finality is purpose.
    And purposes must be.
No act can be without a goal,
    Or else it can't be free.

When purposes are so ignored,
    Confusion soon will follow.
And life that's meant to be so full,
    Turns out to be so hollow.

Most feminists sure miss this point,
    At least that's how it seems.
And so they miss the glory of
    What being woman means.

That's why life is so empty for
    The feminist who bellows.
She truly hates her womanhood,
    And thinks she hates just fellows.

# A RELIGIOUS PEOPLE

Religious beliefs and practices penetrated every phase of life on the African continent. In its primitive societies everything was sacred. Nothing was profane. Everything was holy. African people were deeply religious. The African was totally immersed in religion from before birth until after death. Every action became a kind of ritual, whether it was eating, drinking, planting, hunting, or fishing. The African did not distinguish between the sacred and the secular. The spiritual and the material were one. There were no irreligious Africans.

We must realize in dealing with Africans we are not dealing with a single people. We are dealing with over a thousand nations or tribes speaking over a thousand different languages, inhabiting the earth's second largest continent, a continent much larger than Europe. To further compound the already complicated, Africa's religious beliefs were not universal, but tribal in scope. Each tribe had its own religious system. It is not surprising, then, the concept of God was colored and influenced by the geographical and cultural backgrounds of many individual peoples.

In spite of vast distances between peoples and the barrier of the multiplicity of languages, there was a common concept of God among all Africans. All Africans believed in a Supreme Being who was the origin of all things. He was outside creation, but personally involved in it. In a sense the God of Africans was both transcendent and immanent.

Myths are always careless about details and so there are many unanswered questions and many apparent contradictions in dealing with the particulars of the various African religions. But no matter how they differed one from the other, all religions saw the universe as a seamless whole, from God to the most insignificant speck of dust.

Africans were total monotheists who viewed God as the omnipotent, omniscient and omnipresent supreme being who presided over a realm of lesser divinities and the spirits of departed souls, as well as over a host of animate and inanimate forces residing on earth. Each tribe, from the Ashanti to the Zulu, with myriads between, had its own name for the Supreme Being and its own catalogue of lesser gods. Each had its own account of creation and its own interpretation of death: each had its own myths, legends and fables describing how the creator dealt with his creatures: each had its own individual superstitions and taboos, its own magic and medicine, its own initiation rites and rituals.

We hope to give our readers some knowledge of the variety of African religious thoughts without negating or diminishing in any way the important beliefs held everywhere in common.

# AFRICAN GODS

Where on earth should one begin,
    To treat those ancient gods?
I'll throw their list into the air,
    And try to play the odds.

Ashantis and the Zulu tribes
    A name for God begot,
As did the hunting Pygmy tribe,
    And pastoral Hottentot.

All held some truths in common,
    Like God dwells in the sky,
And he's the source of everything,
    As all tribes testify.

The rain is his most treasured gift,
    For it makes all things grow.
He's blessed men with the oxen
    And water buffalo.

God delegates to lesser gods
    So many little chores.
Especially in creating things,
    A task he so abhors.

Yorubas had their own beliefs,
    Of how all things began.
Their god, Olodumare,
    Had this creative plan.

# A YORUBA CREATION MYTH

What now is earth was once just marsh,
    So very cruel and very harsh.
And up above in heaven's sky,
    God watched with his all-seeing eye.

The marsh was just a place for sport,
    For heaven's guests of every sort.
They all came down a spider's web,
    To hunt and play, the "griot" said.

Where there was marsh God wanted earth,
    So for a builder he made search.
Thus Orisanla got the task.
    "Fill the waste" was what God asked.

God gave him earth within a shell,
    A five-toed hen and bird, as well.
The earth he threw upon the waste.
    The fowls then spread it with great haste.

When this creative work was done,
    God sent his prized chameleon.
It served God as a secret spy,
    Reporting marsh was not quite dry.

# A Yoruba Creation Myth

The sacred spot where work began,
    Was now as wide as eye could scan.
God called it "Ife" meaning "wide."
    And mankind there would first abide.

Four days it took for God's request.
    The fifth day was a day of rest.
Ife would grow into a town,
    And as it grew, it'd reach renown.

God sent a palm tree down to earth,
    And soon mankind would know its worth.
Its fruit gave milk; its seed gave oil.
    Three other trees sprang from the soil.

All these were gifts for future man,
    Conferred on the Yoruba clan.
The hen and bird would multiply,
    And serve as food to satisfy.

Then Orisanla molded man,
    Whom some were black and some were tan.
Olodumare gave man breath,
    Which he would breathe until his death.

Yorubas grew into a tribe,
    Who's glory "griots" would describe.
Fine children came to families blessed,
    The source and goal of happiness.

Wise proverbs were their poetry,
    And teach us their philosophy.
Their riddles speak their special wit,
    Skin drums their messages transmit.

There're many lessons we can learn,
    If from Yorubas we discern.
Their love of children and their past,
    Won't let us play iconoclast.

Deep ties to family were their strength,
    For whom they'd go to any length.
The truths of God were so inbred,
    They lived the way their parents said.

The "rope of life" was in their hand,
    "Unbroken," if they held command.
And for Yorubas this would be,
    A life of generosity.

Protecting both the poor and weak,
    And granting them the love they seek,
Deep reverence for the elderly,
    Avoiding all hypocrisy.

These are some clear derivatives,
    Which we can learn from primitives.
And would that we'd be half as fine,
    So we could read their bottom line.

"Unbroken" then our "rope" must be,
    That binds us to eternity.
May we hold fast that "rope" in hand
    Until we see the "promised land."

Human image from
a Yoruba crown.

# THE ORIGIN OF PYGMIES
## AND BUSHONGOS

A man and woman lived on earth,
    But had no family.
Within their hut there was no mirth.
    No children could one see.

One day Bomazi paid a call,
    And saw their lonely plight.
"Quite soon a child will bless this home,"
    He said with God's foresight.

The couple laughed at promise made,
    For both were now quite old.
But soon unto their lives was born,
    A baby as foretold.

The child grew up a pretty girl,
    Quite filled with zest for life.
Bomazi fell in love with her,
    And took her as his wife.

The twins she bore her lordly spouse,
    She named Woto and Moelo,
Because they were both sons of God,
    Each was a Godly fellow.

# The Origin of Pygmies and Bushongos

Then Woto who had many wives,
  Found one with Moelo's son.
And when he found two more with him,
  His life became undone.

He went into the woods alone,
  And sang among the fig trees.
Then as he sang some dwarfs came forth;
  He had created Pygmies.

He wandered on all by himself.
  Into the woods he trod.
He founded the Bushongo Tribes,
  And Bozami's still their God.

Then many centuries afterwards,
  King Shamba was their chief.
In wisdom he pursued peace's path,
  To spare his tribe war's grief.

Tobacco was his gift to man,
  If such can be a gift.
And oil from palms he introduced,
  An economic lift.

To the Bushongos great fame came,
    A tribe of peace their trait,
Instead of solving feuds by war,
    They'd always mediate.

Perhaps, now what our world needs most,
    Is Shamba pulling strings.
His calm dictates of wisdom's rule
    Make Martin Luther Kings.

# HOW ANCIENT AFRICANS
## VIEWED DEATH

Africans were puzzled by death. They saw death as something deeply mysterious, for it was something totally contrary to the exuberance of life. Yet death struck often and often it seemed senseless, as when it struck the very young or those in the prime of their life.

Africans had many myths to explain death, many beliefs surrounding it, and many rites and rituals accompanying it. They fully understood that death was caused by natural causes like the mortal wound of a poisonous arrow, the bite of a deadly snake, or the attack of some terrible disease. But over and above the natural causes of death, Africans always sought a deeper reason which they judged the real cause. Nothing happened by chance for the African. Effects must have causes. But causes themselves have agents. Africans certainly accepted the scientific explanations of things, but they further wanted to know why such things happened here and now, instead of somewhere else and at another time.

In the face of death a diviner was consulted, not to explain the physical cause of death, but the why of death. Why was this serpent on this path at this time? Why did this disease strike my house? They often found the deeper reason in the curse of witchcraft or the glance of the evil eye.

Various African tribes had various explanations for the ultimate cause of death. The most common explanation was that death was a punishment of God. The Korongo people believed God sent death to punish man for mocking him. A Madagascar myth had the first couple choosing to die themselves so that they could have immortality through children, rather than live forever in loneliness. In many explanations, it was because of women that God sent punishments. A Dogon story spoke of God offering man a cow, if he would be willing to die. The man promptly refused the offer. The same offer was made to his wife. She accepted the cow, even though she never intended to accept death as her part of the bargain. When she returned home her husband was dead. He was the first man to die.

A Sua tale relates that God had forbidden man to look at him. So man did not look, but one of his daughters did. As her punishment, mankind had to forfeit immortality. The Ewe tribe of Togoland explained death as a punishment from God because a woman threw a stone at him. At that time God lived in the lower sky within the sight of man, but once the stone was thrown at him, he withdrew from the lower sky and took up residence beyond the view of man. He sent death as a punishment.

The following piece is a rather interesting explanation of death according to the myths of the Kra tribes.

# A VISIT TO LORD DEATH

The Kra, a tribe in Togoland,
    A dreadful tale did tell,
About a visit to Lord Death,
    Who in their land did dwell.

The visitor was just a boy,
    Who often shared Death's food.
To say that this was foolishness,
    Would prove a platitude.

His brother and his sister, then,
    One day accompanied him.
And what would soon eventuate,
    Is truly rather grim.

They stayed that night at Death's request,
    While brother went back home.
And when he called next day on Death,
    He found just flesh and bone.

The lad in anger struck at Death,
    To kill what killed his kin.
And magically restored their lives,
    Uniting bones to skin.

# A Visit to Lord Death

When he revived his siblings, though,
    His magic touched Death's eye.
That eye now lives and often blinks,
    And then someone must die.

Since death is just a blink away,
    Be careful how you live.
And measure, too, what you receive,
    And what you have to give.

The poor lad eating with Lord Death,
    Was innocent, indeed.
He did not understand at all,
    What give and take concede.

Each time that you accept a gift,
    You somehow go in debt.
And even though the gift's just food,
    You later might regret.

Beware then of indebtedness.
    Some debts are terrifying.
And if that debt is made to death,
    It must be paid by dying.

# RHYTHM IN MUSIC AND DANCE

The African is somehow wedded to rhythm. It is an obsession, a second nature to him; dance and music are its most perfect expressions. Rhythm is the very essence of energy itself. It reflects the nature of the life forces or powers of being. Rhythm reproduces the movements of the human body, which in itself, is in harmony with the movements of man's soul and the movements of the universe. There is rhythm in breathing, rhythm in the beating of the heart, rhythm in walking, rhythm in pounding grain or setting nets. There is rhythm in everything we do, a kind of ebb and flow reflecting the rhythms of the cosmos.

Africans looked upon rhythm as the architect of being. It was rhythm which conferred form and expressed itself in lines, color, and volume in sculpture and painting. It expressed itself in the accent of the stressed and unstressed syllables in poetry, in the rise and fall of notes in music and in the bodily movement of the dance. Prose was turned to poetry by rhythm. In music rhythm took precedence over melody. Rhythm manifested itself most perfectly in the dance. Bodies would tremble, tummies would roll, rear ends would shake and legs would tap.

Solo dancing was rare; so also was the dancing of couples. Dancing was a group activity. The dance more than any other art form reflected African life. There were war dances, victory dances, marriage dances, dances for initiation rites, dances for men, dances for women, dances for both. Like the African folktales, the dance has been handed down from one generation to the next with very little change or alteration. Styles of dance might change from one region to another, but it was always an expression of life — its joys, its fears, its freedoms and its anxieties. Dancers were usually masked and often costumed. Masks were much more than a disguise. They conjured up magic. The wearer was in some way transformed into the being the mask depicted. The mask was empowered with supernatural properties and as such was connected closely with the ritual dance.

Ritual dancing was always serious. It was a religious rite thanking guardian ancestors for their care and concern or praying for rain or harvest. The various rites of initiation were celebrated by dances. By dancing, the hunter sought success in his endeavors or gave thanks for his kill. African dances avoided bodily contact as lower bodies shook in sensuous motion. At times dancing would be frenzied with leapings, stoopings, stompings and jumping all to the throbbing of drums and bells and calabashes. Rhythm was also supplied by chants and clapping. It was this rhythm which gave dancing its form. Without rhythm, music and dance would be crude, without charm or grace. This crudeness would be intolerable to the African.

The love of music, dance and rhythm characterized all African life. These things were obsessions with the African. As their legs were filled with dance and their bodies shook with rhythm, their throats were filled with song. They sang while they planted or harvested. They sang in the mourning of their bereavements. They sang in the joy of their celebrations. Song was a second nature to Africans. Their music, as their art, was rooted in the earth. It expressed feeling. Unless an image was rhythmical it had no affect on the African. In Africa almost every word was descriptive. Everything was a sign. To a great extent, this signification was brought about by rhythm. To accomplish this, rhythm used a constant repetition of facts, actions, songs and words. Nowhere has rhythm and repetition reigned more despotically than in Africa.

The African's obsession with rhythm in music and dance is clearly portrayed in the following folktale. It accounts for the reason spiders now have humps. As the reader will discover in this bit of doggerel, spiders were not always ugly. They were once the most handsome of creatures. They were the envy of all life forms in the universe. No longer is that the case. All has changed because of the events described in the following.

# WHY SPIDERS HAVE HUMPS

There was a time when spiders were
 The handsomest of creatures.
And women here and everywhere,
 Were spellbound by their features.

Anansee was the most renown,
 Of all the spider race.
And women came from near and far,
 To see his noble face.

His dress was most impeccable,
 His manners debonair.
His speech was soft and sensuous,
 And what a "derriere."

So women walked for many moons,
 To capture his attention.
They named their babies after him,
 And did things we won't mention.

He loved to dance more than the dwarfs,
 And sing more than the birds.
This proved to be his downfall when,
 Love turned to deeds and words.

# Why Spiders Have Humps

The dwarfs sang songs and did their dance
    Around the clock each night.
But they forbade that anyone
    Should join in their delight.

The dwarfs were hunchbacked, little men,
    Who loved their dance and song.
If others tried to chisel in,
    "Dwarf humps" repaid the wrong.

A hump would grow in punishment,
    On backs of those who'd dance.
So kids were early warned of this,
    Lest they would dance by chance.

But rhythm filled Anansee's blood,
    Which put him in a trance.
When dwarfs beat on their tom-tom drums,
    He simply had to dance.

So up and down this spider jumped
    To frenzied drummer's beat.
For when he heard the drummer's call,
    He had to move his feet.

He asked the dwarfs if he could join
    Their nightly tribal rite.
They said as long as dwarfs were there,
    They thought it'd be all right.

But when the dwarfs would finish,
    And go back to their huts,
He, too, would have to call it quits,
    No ifs, no ands, no buts.

If he would disobey this rule,
    They'd have to counteract.
By dwarf's decree he soon would grow
    A hump upon his back.

Anansee danced with Dwarfs that night.
    The dwarfs retired at dawn.
The spider could not stop his feet,
    They had to carry on.

Besides he didn't believe their threats
    About the ugly hump.
So when the dwarfs retired to bed,
    He stayed to dance and jump.

# Why Spiders Have Humps

"A woman and a melody,
    Who can resist their charm?
Since both are so desirable,
    Why should they cause one harm?"

The sun when it arose that day,
    Became the first beholder,
That proud Anansee now possessed
    A hump upon his shoulder.

With mounds of flesh upon his back,
    He could not stand up straight.
He ordered it to go away,
    But now it was too late.

He dug a hole into the floor,
    And laid down on his back.
He fit his bump into the hole,
    Which fit just like a sack.

When wives came in to fix a meal
    To feed their handsome mate,
They pulled at him until they saw
    The hump that was his fate.

Then all his wives and harem left,
     Without a kiss or hug,
For he who once reigned handsomely.
     Was now an ugly bug.

Quite soon the village heard the tale
     About Anansee's grief.
The passing glories of this world,
     Most surely can be brief.

So do not place your hope in things,
     That simply will not last.
For life will topple worldly toys,
     And play iconoclast.

Learn from the ugly spider then.
     Don't dance to this world's tune.
For when the world collects its debt,
     No one can be immune.

I believe that blacks are far more wise
     Than others of our age.
They've learned from ugly spiders that
     The world is just a stage.

# Why Spiders Have Humps

We've crossed that stage so many times,
    And plaudits came our way.
But Africans are wise enough,
    To know that they don't stay.

They know this from their history,
    Which brought them wealth and fame,
Which then were stolen from their race,
    When Europeans came.

Then they who treasured freedom's path,
    Were sold as worthless slaves,
And taken from the land they loved,
    By money-hungry knaves.

They first enslaved blacks physically,
    And then enslaved their mind,
They robbed them of their heritage,
    To which most now are blind.

These white men forced their ways on them,
    As blacks have now discerned.
The worldly values white men lived,
    The black men quickly learned.

But black men would be foolish, if
    They put aside their past,
And pitched their culture's heritage,
    Without a question asked.

The foolish spider was confused,
    Perhaps he was insane.
He tried to be what he was not,
    And that's what he became.

He traded off nobility,
    To live like little men.
Accepting what they offered him,
    Became his greatest sin.

When greatness wished to be a dwarf,
    A dwarf it then became.
And if the black man wishes this,
    He, too, must be insane.

Let no man trade his culture's gifts,
    Nor values that they gave
By giving up the things you love,
    You soon become a slave.

# LIFE IN THE BUSH

Africans had a deep appreciation of mental keenness. They had a sympathy and admiration for those who used their wits to extract themselves from difficult situations. They had no patience nor pity for those who failed to use their brains to avoid or escape annoying predicaments. Those who outwitted opponents were respected more than those who outfought them. Cleverness was a trait much revered in African folktales. People never tired of tales in which heroes outwitted opponents, no matter how detailed or repetitive the story might be. They were never in a hurry to get to the conclusion of a story as their Europeans counterparts might be. They loved the details in stories involving wit or riddle.

Life in the bush required common sense just to survive. This challenge of daily survival was like a riddle and served as a basic theme of African oral literature. No one knows the origin of these tales, but they absorb and distill the essence of African life. They relate African culture to daily living: what they eat, how they dress, how they think and feel and believe. Through folktales the world is given an unclouded view of daily life and customs of the Africa of the past. This account alone should do much to dispel the unfortunate misconception that Africa had no values worthy of the world's admiration or worthy of the world's imitation. Africans loved riddles. Often their values are depicted in riddle form which the unwitting fail to understand.

# A TALE OF ANANSEE'S TRIALS
## IN THE BUSH

For three long years there was no rain.
The rivers turned to puddles.
Savanna grass no longer grew,
And men grew quite befuddled.

All fetishes had failed to lure
Clouds back into the sky.
A famine spread throughout the land,
As men and beasts did die.

Anansee, too, felt hunger pangs,
With cramps and dizzy spells.
There was no food, no fruit, no grain,
Nor nuts found in their shells.

So spider got his fishing pole,
And set about to fish.
He hoped that he could catch some food
To put upon his dish.

For many days he fished and fished,
But no fish were in sight.
No matter what he used for bait,
He never got a bite.

He simply could not catch a fish,
But still he kept on trying.
A swallow then flew off to God,
To tell him men were dying.

As soon as God was told the news,
A fish jumped from the brook.
It headed for Anansee's pole,
And landed on his hook.

The little fish began to cry,
"Please, spider, spare my life.
I'll give you every happiness,
And spare you every strife."

This trickster spider often used
Deception just as quick.
And so he didn't believe the fish,
Whose promise seemed a trick.

"I'll prove it if you'll climb this tree,
And jump down to the ground.
Then all the joys you'd ever want
Will instantly be found."

# A Tale of Anansee's Trials in the Bush

Anansee finally acquiesced,
    Despite the heights he feared.
He climbed, he jumped, he landed,
    And happiness appeared.

His favorite foods were everywhere,
    A French gourmet's cuisine.
And when the famine left the land,
    He was knighted by the queen.

She made him her prime minister,
    With one thing very clear.
"What ere you wish, feel free to do,
    But don't look in my mirror."

"No, do not look into my mirror.
    That is my one command.
I know you think this foolishness,
    But try to understand."

Anansee wondered why this rule.
    The mirror must be magic.
If he would miss this golden chance,
    It truly would be tragic.

The spider then sought out the mirror,
    To see what it'd deliver.
And instantly he found himself
    Back fishing at the river.

Again he felt those hunger pangs,
    That he had known before.
Regretting then his foolish greed,
    He hoped for one encore.

Just then he hooked another fish.
    Fate must be on his side.
Now that he had a second chance,
    He'd not be greedy-eyed.

So, quickly he addressed the fish:
    "Should I do the same again?"
"Do what you wish." the fish replied,
    Then splashed and said, "Amen."

The spider quickly climbed the tree,
    And hurled himself to earth.
He bruised himself but did not die,
    That's why this yarn has worth.

# A Tale of Anansee's Trials in the Bush

There's such finality in death!
    What else can it allot?
So if a death had happened here,
    There'd be no counterplot.

But as it is, the tale lives on,
    And often is retold,
As riddle or a test of sense,
    Retold a thousandfold.

It's now a tale of inquiry,
    To see what you would do,
How you would act if you were in
    That silly spider's shoe.

For we are all confronted with
    Forbidden mirrors in life.
And though we think we need each one,
    They only cause us strife.

So do not seek forbidden fruit,
    Or mirrors which destroy.
But be content with what you are,
    And what you are enjoy.

Most Africans were simple folks,
    Who found joy in their home.
This story pointed out to them,
    The price one pays to roam.

No meddling curiosity,
    Possessed the black man's thought.
If there were love within his home,
    He had all that he sought.

Blacks saw a seamless universe,
    From God to grain of sand.
The family was its focal point,
    But family was the clan.

The clan embraced all relatives,
    Those living and those dead,
Not just a mom and dad and kids,
    Like Europeans said.

The family was the vital force
    The source of life and hope.
And if one's taken from its strength,
    He simply cannot cope.

And this is just what happened,
    Through slavery's mortal wrong.
Then due to white men's pride and greed,
    Those wrongs have been prolonged.

# A Tale of Anansee's Trials in the Bush

It takes some time to counteract,
    A trauma that is deep.
And if it happens to a race,
    That's cause for it to weep.

For when men brood or hold a grudge,
    Their actions will destroy them.
They must be taught their racial strengths,
    If they are to enjoy them.

Traditions build tomorrow's hopes,
    And keep them from the looter.
That's why tradition must be taught;
    And be a black youth's tutor.

The strength and love in black men's homes,
    Which marked their native land,
Must be retaught to present youth,
    For greatness to expand.

These are the things young blacks must learn
    As Cosby clearly teaches.
And when they learn, they will excel.
    Learn well, the world beseeches.

# A CHOICE AND A RIDDLE

A hunter who was very poor,
    Set out his traps in vain.
Then after weeks of nothing caught,
    A boa he constrained.

Intending to destroy the snake,
    The hunter lifted spear.
The serpent then addressed him,
    And spoke in words quite clear.

"Oh, please, don't kill me, hunter.
    Just free me from your net.
And all the wealth you'd ever want,
    I'll guarantee you'll get."

"Release me and you soon shall be
    The richest man on earth.
No man could ever count your gold
    Or estimate your worth."

The hunter hesitated long.
    Why should he believe a snake?
But then he mused with greed's desire,
    What there could be at stake.

# A Choice and a Riddle

The hunter then released the snake,
    Which said: "Please, follow me."
The two set out to gather what
    The snake had guaranteed.

Through forests of the boas,
    They journeyed cross great streams,
Where genies played and breezes sang,
    And things weren't what they seemed.

This was the land where boas lived.
    Here years seemed but a day.
There was such peace and happiness,
    That hunter hoped to stay.

But he had come in quest for gold,
    And now, in turn, must go.
He took with him two magic gourds,
    Which boa did bestow.

"Throw one gourd to the ground when home,
    But listen to the other.
You'll understand whatever speaks,
    As if it were your brother."

At home he did as he was told,
    And threw the gourd to ground.
A golden castle came to be,
    And golden treasures found.

The hunter had a hunting dog,
    The dog a mangy friend.
The two spoke of a famine,
    That soon would there descend.

The hunter heard and understood
    The words each dog had said.
When famine came, he was prepared;
    His family was well fed.

The mangy dog next said to friend:
    "Soon village girls will die.
To those who dwell across the stream,
    My words do not apply."

The hunter heard and moved his home
    Across the stream of water.
A plague then struck and all girls died,
    All but his lovely daughter.

The mangy dog said to his friend:
   "Your master is unique.
I think he truly understands
   The language that we speak."

A lot of other things occurred
   That justified his theory.
But after many years had passed,
   The man with age grew weary.

The mangy dog said to his friend:
   "Your master soon will die."
"Can he be saved?" his own dog asked,
   "Or must I say good-bye?"

"He can be saved if he returns
   The gourds which were the snake's.
But then a pauper he will be,
   If treasures he forsakes."

"When will this death befall him?
   When must he pay its debt?"
"It will be soon, this very day.
   He'll die when sun has set."

The hunter heard these dreadful words,
    As sun climbed in the sky.
He knew that he would have to chose
    To be poor or to die.

The more he thought about his wealth,
    The more his wealth possessed him.
Each time he tried to give gourds back,
    The more his wealth caressed him.

His wives were working cheerfully;
    His children were at play.
The sun had reached its apex now;
    He could not long delay.

"Does not your master know that he
    Is now about to die?"
"He must, for I have noticed that
    There's sadness in his eye."

"I doubt he has the courage to
    Abandon all his wealth.
But what are riches when compared
    To living or to health."

# A Choice and a Riddle

The sun was getting lower now,
    As dogs put up a bet.
Would hunter choose past poverty
    Before the sun would set?

The dogs both laughed as hunter stewed,
    About which choice to make.
The wealthy man was poor, indeed.
    Whichever he'd forsake.

The foolish man relied on things.
    His values were confused.
With all his opportunities,
    He could not be excused.

The shadows were beneath the trees.
    His time was running out.
He hesitated as he paced.
    His choice was still in doubt.

The story ended in that vein.
    And left the choice to you.
If you had lived that hunter's life,
    What is it you would do?

# The Wisdom of African Mythology

How long would you still hesitate,
    Before you made your choice?
If it had been immediate,
    I think you should rejoice.

But if your choice was long delayed,
    Or you chose death to life,
Your values are indeed confused,
    Not knowing joy from strife.

In each of us there is a bit,
    Of judgment hesitation.
When faced with options, we reflect
    The hunter's desperation.

Such hesitance should clearly teach
    That something is amiss.
So hope that you will never hear
    An ambushed python's hiss.

Or if you do, don't let him out,
    Whatever else you do.
Just take your knife and skin the snake,
    Before that snake skins you.

# TABOOS

One cannot read much of African myths or delve into them deeply until one is confronted with taboos and prohibitions of every kind. Such taboos traced their origin to mythical legends. The Africans ate a wide variety of meat. They ate animals and insects of every sort and size. Yet there were certain animals they would not eat. The killing of certain animals was strictly forbidden due to taboos which entered their mythical history somewhere along the way.

The king of Iba had an interfering wife. She entered his council meetings and tried to dominate and dictate tribal affairs. The tribal elders were displeased and used obscene words to show their disapproval. The king was so embarrassed and ashamed of his meddlesome wife that he fled into the forest never to be seen again. Each section of the village then elected its own chieftain. When the high king, the Oba of Benin, heard what had happened (thinking the village had deposed its king) he sent his armies to the village to destroy the people. The villagers hid in the forest when they heard the soldiers coming.

When the king's army entered the village, the soldiers saw the paw prints of bush rats leaving the town and thought the people had fled. At the other end of the village they saw the footprints of antelopes exiting the village at that end. Now the army was certain that the villagers had abandoned their town, and so the soldiers left the territory and no one was punished. To this very day, out of gratitude, the people of Iba do not eat bush rats or antelopes. Their killing is taboo.

Folktales have been described as "little novels of childlike intellects." Africans spoke of life and its goals by telling stories, not by an integrated philosophy. Their tales included stories of almost every kind of animal. By narrating the animal's peculiarities and behavioral traits, moral lessons were usually taught, and often times most clearly.

There was a time when all the animals lived together as members of a single family in a wonderful garden of peace and tranquility. However, the sins or tricks of the spider and the thievery of the hyena broke up that happy home. Rivalries replaced friendships. Doubts replaced trust, as credulity gave way to deceit. Discord and death superseded the harmony of jungle life. The world of myth now fell before the world of reality.

# THE PIG'S TRUNK

There was a time in days gone by,
    When pigs possessed a trunk.
It made the pig most beautiful,
    And also quite a hunk.

This trunk they had in place of snout
    Was powerful and big.
It made the jungle's governor
    The rather lowly pig.

The elephants were envious.
    That pigs had such prestige.
So soon all pigs were victims of
    A pachydermic siege.

These elephants were saddened that
    The pig's trunk was so fine,
That bushmen treasured elephants
    Less than some porcupine.

The spiders, too, were envious
    That pigs had been so gifted,
For spiders, known for cleverness,
    Now saw that glory shifted.

# The Wisdom of African Mythology

There had been seven jungle beasts
    Considered noble beings.
The pachyderms were number one,
    With no one disagreeing.

The rhinos, lions and buffaloes,
    Next took their place in line.
Then other cats filled in the ranks
    With spiders far behind.

These animals had made a pact,
    To help each other out.
And whether it be day or night,
    They'd help without a doubt.

Small animals all lived in fear.
    They shook when lions roared.
Or when they heard the panther's paw,
    They fled in disaccord.

But all these noble animals,
    Now feared the gentle pig,
Not due to its ferocity,
    But to its trunk so big.

## The Pig's Trunk

One day the spider had a dream,
    About a large-nosed genie,
Its size was like a hundred trees,
    While spiders were so teeny.

When spider woke up from his nap,
    He had but one desire,
A nose just like that Genie had
    He simply must acquire.

For with the nose that Genie had
    As hunter he'd be best.
When people spoke of cleverness,
    It's he they would suggest.

His nose would be a constant threat
    To every other beast.
The trunks of pigs would fade away
    To second place, at least.

The spider then composed a nose
    From noses of the dead,
And with the help of all his kids,
    Attached it to his head.

So thinking now that he was king,
    He riled some buffaloes.
But when he tried to ward them off,
    He couldn't lift his nose.

To save himself the spider hid
    Within a deep black hole.
Discarding nose, he burrowed in
    As if he were a mole.

Once there he felt that he was safe
    From all who now despised him.
But then the long-trunked pig came by,
    Whose long trunk soon surprised him.

One time this evil spider ate
    The piglets of this pig.
So when these others sought his help,
    The pig would not renege.

He stuck his trunk into the hole
    To take the spider's life.
But when the trunk was deep within,
    It met a red-hot knife.

# The Pig's Trunk

The spider cut the pig's trunk off,
    And only left a snout.
And this is what the pig's friends saw,
    When nose was lifted out.

The trunk was left inside the hole,
    Which spiders quickly ate.
And to this day all pigs just have
    A snout to compensate.

This African tale teaches us
    A lesson we should learn.
If pigs or spiders we become,
    We surely shall get burned.

If we like pigs stick noses in,
    Where they do not belong,
It won't be very long until,
    Some one will do us wrong.

And when we pull our noses out,
    Whence they should not have been,
We'll be embarrassed and we'll blush,
    And wear a sheepish grin.

# The Wisdom of African Mythology

At least we would if we had learned,
    From all our past misdeeds.
But if we do not feel ashamed,
    Then decency recedes.

In some way white men of the past
    Have acted just that way.
Colonialism in Africa,
    Is white man's expose.

Whites stole black ways and history
    And treasures unsurpassed.
And left behind utility,
    A value that can't last.

Nor have those whites apologized,
    Or felt their actions wrong.
They tell blacks they've been civilized.
    And sing the same old song.

But once they lift their sinless heads,
    Long buried in the sands,
They'll have to face those evil deeds,
    Done by their greedy hands.

# The Pig's Trunk

And as they acted like the pig,
 So spider's way they chose,
Enlarging white predominance,
 As spider did its nose.

The spider used another's death
 To further its own goal.
It cared not what it trampled on,
 If it could gain control.

As spiders gather everything
 Within their evil web,
The whites felt if their tide could rise,
 All other tides should ebb.

The spider and the long-trunked pig,
 Teach clearly by this tale.
No matter what another's greed,
 God's justice will prevail.

Apologizing, whites should be
 Ashamed and sensitive.
And black men with their heads held high
 Should say that they forgive.

# WHY TURTLES HAVE CRACKED SHELLS

A famine struck all Africa.
    Its food supply had vanished.
And as it lasted many months,
    The animals were famished.

The younger ones then made a pact,
    So they could get some meat.
They gruesomely decided that
    Their mothers they would eat.

To bite the hand that gives you food,
    Is rude to say the least.
But he who eats his mom for food,
    Must be the world's worst beast.

The squirrel could not bring himself
    To eat someone he loved.
He took his mother to the sky,
    And hid her up above.

When hungry he would sing a chant
    And she'd let down a rope.
He climbed to her and ate his fill,
    Of nuts and cantaloupe.

# Why Turtles Have Cracked Shells

The other beasts discovered this,
    But never said a word.
But when the squirrel was out of sight,
    They sang the chant they'd heard.

The rope descended to the earth.
    The tortoise took a hold.
He gradually was lifted up,
    As it had been foretold.

The little squirrel came back in time
    To sing a counter song.
His mother quickly cut the rope,
    For something must be wrong.

And when the rope was cut in two,
    The brazen tortoise fell.
A victim of deceitfulness,
    He badly smashed his shell.

A little snail then took some paste,
    And glued it back together.
That's why the turtle's shell now looks
    Like cracked and checkered leather.

# The Wisdom of African Mythology

These Africans would long discuss,
    Why things are as they are,
Why snakes change skins and pigs have snouts
    And turtle shells are scarred.

These tales became a history
    Of wise and ancient thought.
They clearly handed down to us
    The lessons wisdom taught.

They teach us we should question things,
    And ask the reason why.
And when that answer has been found,
    We might eat humble pie.

So many answers we've been taught
    Aren't really deep enough.
What scientists today conclude,
    Tomorrow's will rebuff.

So much we claim we know, we don't.
    We're less wise than we think.
In thought we'll travel just so far,
    But never cross the brink.

# Why Turtles Have Cracked Shells

That's why the ancients wisely said:
  "Cross over, go beyond.
Please, listen to what nature  says,
  And with your mind respond."

Book learning takes you just so far,
  But that's not far enough.
Somehow you must go on your own,
  And call book learning's bluff.

# AN EARFUL OF MOSQUITOES

A pretty ear once held a test,
   To chose who'd marry her.
Contestants took their place in line,
   To see whom she'd prefer.

A cute mosquito came with hope.
   That he would be her choice.
He hummed and buzzed to charm the ear,
   But she ignored his voice.

Dismissed as insignificant,
   The poor bug was offended.
He could not woo that pretty ear
   On which he had descended.

He sadly left with feelings hurt,
   But he will reappear.
To prove he's not a fly by night,
   He still will buzz the ear.

The ear finds him annoying now.
   But that's just what he seeks.
No longer insignificant,
   Ears listen when he speaks.

## An Earful of Mosquitoes

I'm sure that all of us have felt,
    Rejected as was he.
And like him, too, our vengeance waits
    The opportunity.

The Africans within our land,
    Know that mosquito's feelings.
They came in search of wedding feasts,
    But got just double-dealings.

They could not woo society,
    Nor golf at country clubs.
They could not eat in white cafes,
    Nor drink in white men's pubs.

They first were insignificant,
    But then became annoying.
Whites found them rather useful, though,
    In "bootlicking" employing.

But like mosquitoes blacks returned,
    For justice, not revenge,
And now that white men know their worth,
    Past wrongs make white men twinge.

But still blacks don't get half a chance,
    Except in all the sports.
But if they had that chance they'd win,
    In life as on the courts.

They've learned well from mosquitoes, though,
    To buzz and bother ears.
This forces whites to recognize,
    Blacks must possess careers.

# WHY AFRICANS ARE SATISFIED WITH WHAT THEY ARE

There were four men who lived on earth.
    Each had his type of toil,
One chased, one trapped, one searched for fruit.
    The fourth one tilled the soil.

Each was unhappy with his life,
    And wanted God to change it.
Each wished to do what others did,
    And asked God to arrange it.

God told them he was busy then,
    Preparing food to eat.
He asked if they could come again,
    When he'd have time to meet.

Before they left God gave them rice
    To hold 'til they returned.
They took the rice indifferently,
    Then left quite unconcerned.

The first saw game and dropped the rice
    To hunt the game he'd seen.
The second, seeing birds to trap,
    Dropped rice for fowl's cuisine.

The third man dropped the rice God gave,
    While reaching for some fruit.
The fourth man lost the rice he had,
    While digging for a root.

When these men called on God again,
    God asked them for the rice.
Each one told God what had occurred,
    And hoped excuse sufficed.

God told them that this lesson taught
    That fate could not be changed,
That each of them would always be
    What nature had arranged.

The hunter would be happiest,
    When he was hunting game.
The trapper needed nets and traps,
    Fulfillment to attain.

The gatherer must gather fruit,
    To give his life full worth.
The farmer, for contentedness,
    Must always till the earth.

# Why Africans are Satisfied with What They Are

So each went back to what he was,
　　But now was satisfied.
He thought he wanted something else,
　　But had been jaundiced-eyed.

The grass is greener, so they say,
　　Beyond your neighbor's fence.
But if you're on your neighbor's side,
　　The green is less intense.

I'm sure there are some black men now,
　　Who wish that they were white.
But if this would eventuate,
　　I'm sure they'd be contrite.

The difficulties that we have
　　Might cause us much chagrin.
But rest assured, they're not caused by
　　The color of our skin.

They're mostly due to attitudes,
　　Of others or ourselves,
Those attitudes of ignorance,
　　That flow from fools themselves.

For when a man is ignorant,
    He's quick to ridicule.
He thinks he is a Solomon,
    But really is a fool.

Be proud of what you have been born,
    Of gifts your mother gave.
Your ancestors were priceless men,
    In spite of being slaves.

One's color's unimportant,
    An accidental thing.
It's what's within your soul that counts
    It's that which makes you king.

# THE ORIGIN OF FIRE

From ancient times man has been puzzled by the origin of fire. All men of past ages agreed that fire originally came from their gods, sometimes as a gift of divine kindness to man, or sometimes through the misdeeds of man who stole it from God, as in the case of Prometheus in Greek Mythology. Both of these explanations are found in African Mythologies.

The Ila tribes claimed fire was brought from heaven by the mason-wasp, the most common insect in Africa. The mason-wasp builds mud nests on walls or curtains. It lays its eggs, puts in grubs to feed them, and then disappears. It never sees its young once they are born. The mason-wasp is most often found near the fireplace, and so Ila people claim that it was this insect which first brought fire from heaven. It flew to God and begged for fire so that creatures on earth could stay warm. God rewarded the efforts of this insect by declaring that the mason-wasp in the future would be over all the birds and insects of Africa.

The Pygmies of the Congo forests say they were the first to have fire, and later it came to the Negroes who thought they were masters over the Pygmies. Once when a Pygmy was chasing an elephant, he arrived at the very village of God and saw a fire burning. He grabbed a piece of it and ran off. God caught him and made him bring it back. Three times this happened and then finally God made a fence around his village to keep out the intruding pygmy.

The pygmy jumped the fence and saw God's mother sleeping near the fire. He stole the fire and brought it back to earth. God's mother awoke due to the cold and called her son. By the time her son arrived at the village his mother had died from the cold. God then declared that although man now had fire, he now must die.

Another pygmy tale states it was the chimpanzees that originally possessed fire. A pygmy visited the village of the chimps, sat around their fire, and wondered how he could steal it. One day he visited their village dressed in bark cloth, he sat by their fire and ate the bananas they gave him. He was so close to the fire that his clothing started to smolder.

The chimps warned him. He told them not to worry and moved closer to the fire. When his clothing caught on fire he ran away heading for his village. The chimps chased after him, but by the time they caught him in his village, there were fires everywhere. They scolded the pygmy and went home grumbling. Ever since then, chimps have abandoned their village and moved into forests without fires and without bananas.

The Dogon people also have a myth about the origin of fire. The following folk tale relates the Dogon idea of the origin of fire and why, according to the Dogon tribes, all men have joints at the elbows and knees.

# FIRE AND JOINTS

Man's ancestors were Nummo spirits
   All sons of God by birth.
They were employed as heaven's smiths
   But lived down here on earth.

When they first dwelled outside of heaven
   They had no fire to warm them.
Their life was cold and very bleak.
   And cold they knew would harm them.

Then one of them went to the sun,
   And stole a piece of fire.
He placed it in a leather belt,
   Before he would expire.

The other Nummos saw the deed,
   And tried to stop the theft.
One threw a lightning bolt at him,
   Which passed him on the left.

Another threw a thunderbolt.
   It also missed its mark.
Since no one could restrain the thief,
   He stole and disembarked.

He headed for the rainbow's bridge,
    And slid to earthly ground,
He hit the earth so very hard
    His fractures were compound.

With knees and elbows busted up,
    It took much time to heal.
But now that he had heaven's fire,
    At least its warmth he'd feel.

Since then all men who walk this earth,
    Who from that Nummo came,
Have joints in elbows and in knees,
    The price they've paid for flame.

I think all life is still somewhat
    Like what the Nummo found,
As he slid down the rainbow's rays,
    And landed on the ground.

We still slide down the rainbow's beam,
    And sometimes go unmarred.
But often as we reach its end,
    We bounce a bit too hard.

I think this is especially true,
    When dreams have long been dreamed.
For when we face reality,
    Those dreams aren't what they seemed.

And then like Nummos we will get
    Completely out of joint,
For dreams anticipated long,
    So often disappoint.

# THE ORIGIN OF DARKNESS

When God first made the universe,
   All things were warm and bright.
The sun gave light throughout the day,
   The moon throughout the night.

Both cold and darkness were unknown,
   When this world first began.
And that's the way it still would be,
   If bats obeyed God's plan.

God gave a basket to a bat
   To carry to the moon.
The sum of darkness was within,
   But proved inopportune.

The bat flew off to find the moon,
   With darkness as its freight.
It stopped to rest along the way,
   For it was getting late.

It put the basket on the ground
   And went in search for food.
Some animals then happened by
   Inquisitive in mood.

They set about to check things out,
  And lifted basket's lid.
The plan of God that had prevailed
  These animals undid.

The bat flew back, but not in time,
  The future had been shaped.
For when the basket was unsealed,
  God's darkness had escaped.

Since that unfortunate event,
  The bat now sleeps all day.
At night it travels off again
  To seek what's gone astray.

It tries to find what it has lost
  To bring it to the moon.
One day, I'm sure, it will succeed,
  But that will not be soon.

The bat's life is an endless quest
  To find where darkness landed.
To carry it unto the moon,
  And do what God commanded.

Again we see the Africans,
    Astutely asking why.
Why darkness comes and why at night,
    Great bats fly in the sky.

# AFRICAN PROVERBS

The use of proverbs to enliven discourse was an indispensable tool in African folklore. This was especially true among the Yoruba tribes. Their many proverbs were, in some way, their national poetry. A nation's proverbs embody an entire ethics. They are observations of a country's manners and morals. Proverbs were as much a part of African life as were riddles. Both were employed by the Griot to teach and to entertain.

We find many of Africa's proverbs similar to those found in other lands and among other people. They are often paraphrases one of the other. There are many examples of this. For instance, the African proverb: "Mouth not keeping to mouth and lip not keeping to lip bring trouble to the jaw," we find paraphrased in the familiar proverb: "Talk is silver, silence is gold."

In the following little verses I have tried to keep the meaning of some ancient African proverbs while transposing their words into a kind of doggerel poetry.

## SOME WOLOF PROVERBS

"What children say,
　　They've heard at home."
So watch your tongue,
　　Its slanders roam.

"Know yourself better
　　Than does he,
The one who often
　　Speaks of thee."

"If the beginning's
　　Known quite well,
On the conclusion
　　You need not dwell."

"To love a king
　　Makes him your debtor."
If he loves you,
　　It's even better.

"Without your fingers
　　Your hand would be
A spoon." Perhaps,
　　By God's decree.

"Running about
    Will make no scholar."
So calm the student,
    By a holler.

"The woman who
    Has lost her rival,
Is very happy
    In her survival."

"Before you try
    To heal others.
First heal yourself."
    And then your brothers.

"The teeth of man
    Serve as a fence,"
For his loud mouth,
    And its offense.

"A runaway dog
    Then has no Master,"
And this can be
    A great disaster.

"The man who says
  "Give all away,"
Deserves your thanks"
  Without delay.

"Time will destroy
  Most everything."
Both love and hate,
  And what they bring.

"Children will hate
  All those who give
All things to them"
  'Cept how to live.

"If there is cause
  To hate someone,
The cause to love
  Has just begun."

"Before one shoots,
  A man must aim."
And those who don't,
  Will bring on shame.

"Man's provisions
　　All will end."
And that is when
　　You need a friend.

"Talk but little
　　And listen much."
For wisdom is
　　The likes of such.

"If chin's too long,
　　You cannot kiss."
And if you try,
　　You'll only miss.

"He who can do
　　Nothing at all
Will never walk."
　　Nor will he crawl.

"Nothing suffices
　　Except that which
Man does not have,"
　　For it he'll itch.

"Before you eat,
    Open your mouth."
Before you search,
    Determine south.

"It is better to walk
    Than curse the road."
You'll always lose
    If you explode.

"Rising early
    Makes the road short."
Time always is
    Your best support.

Part of a purification rite mask
from Bobo of Upper Volta

"A tree not taller
    Than an ant
Cannot shade you."
    No, it can't.

"If a woman
    Speaks two words,
Take but one."
    The other's absurd.

"One does not love,
    If one does not
Accept from others,"
    What they've got.

"The pillar of
    The world is hope."
Reject it and
    You'll always grope.

"Hold a true friend
    With both hands."
Of this world's treasures,
    None's more grand.

## OJI PROVERBS

"When your mouth stumbles,
    It's worse than feet."
It proves your brains
    Are obsolete.

"That man's a fool
    Whose sheep flees twice."
The poor old fellow
    Needs more advice.

## ACCRA PROVERBS

"Anger's removed
    By some good word."
It disappears;
    Or so I've heard.

"To warn a man
    Is not to scold him."
If sound advice
    Is what you've told him.

"Remove the elephant
     From the forest.
And buffalo's stock
     Really soarest."

"He who marries
     A real beauty,
Is seeking trouble,"
     From his cutie.

"He who asks
     The fool to dance
Is no better"
     Unless by chance.

"Strife never begets
     A gentle child."
But peace begets
     A child that's mild.

"Inquiry saves
     A man from error."
But apathy
     Will cause him terror.

"In our own eyes
    We all are good."
So I wonder why
    There's spinsterhood.

"Competition
    And reward
As inducements
    Beat the cord."

"Fall by your feet
    You'll rise again.
Fall by your mouth,
    You're down for ten."

"There is no medicine
    Against old age."
But living long
    Makes man a sage.

"The young can't teach
    Traditions to the old."
And those who try,
    Are surely bold.

"Peace is the father
    Of friendship's righting.
Wrong doing's father
    Of bitter fighting."

"Aggressive men
    Will die in wars."
And drinking men
    Will die in bars.

"It's food we eat that
    Fills our bellies."
So portly men eat
    Lots of jellies.

"The proverb is
    'The horse' of speech."
So use it often
    When you teach.

Adopt the wisdom
    Of each poem,
Before the author
    Writes his own.

Each proverb is
    An African jewel.
The stuff you'll never
    Learn in school.

Baoule gold wire mask
pendant worn by royalty

# TOTEMS

Totemism and animal stories make up a great part of African Mythology. African folktales, like most folktales everywhere, were meant to instruct as well as please. Totemism existed everywhere throughout the Africa that was south of the Sahara. It played a very important role in the Mythologies of that part of Africa.

A totem was a class of material objects which native Africans regarded with a superstitious respect. They believed between themselves and every member of that class, there existed an intimate and special relationship. The connection between a man and his totem was beneficial to both. The totem protected the man and the man paid respect to the totem in a variety of ways. If his totem were an animal, he would not kill it; if it were a plant or a tree, he would not cut it down or gather any of it its fruit.

Totems were distinguished from fetishes in that a fetish was an isolated, individual thing, while a totem was never an individual thing, but always a whole class of things. Sometimes totems were inanimate objects like carvings or artifacts. Some totems were natural elements like the sun or the rain. Others were animate beings like animals or insects. The Barolong tribe had a totem of iron. At one time their totem was the kidu. They would not kill it or eat its flesh. Once, in a time of famine, a kidu was killed by someone accidentally. No one dared eat it, although people were starving. The tribal chief then changed the totem from the kidu to the iron spear that killed it.

The animals most figured in totems were the hare, the tortoise, the spider, the antelope, the jackal, the chameleon, the elephant, the lion and the hyena. The transformation of men into animals or animals into men was common in African folklore. Totems were not worshipped in any real sense. The relationship was one of friendship with others who possessed the same totem. They were related like animals of the same species.

At times totemism developed into worship of the animal or plant. Totemism sometimes developed into a zoolatry. The Baganda tribes had a "python-god," Selwanga, whose temple was in Budu. The Wawangas had sacred rites to the python. Straw images of serpents were often seen stuck in the ground. The Ewe tribes had three totems, the python, the crocodile, and the leopard. They all became tribal deities. Totemism did not involve believing in re-incarnation in the form of the carved animal in one's totem. Totemism always included the class, never the individual. The Wachaga people considered baboons, pythons and elephants their totems.

Many believed they were descended from their totem. The story is told of a Wachaga girl from the Wakonadai clan who was forced to marry a man from the Wakosalema clan against her will. She then refused to eat food and subsisted on grass and leaves and eventually turned into an elephant and escaped into the forest. She returned to feed on her own peoples' gardens. The Wakonadai clan never harmed one of their own, but after that, if they met someone from the Wakoselma clan they instantly killed him.

The Nandi people had a clan whose totem was the bee, another whose totem was the baboon, and another whose totem was the leopard. But those clans whose totem was the hyena had special privileges and were highly esteemed. All Nandi tribes respected the hyena. Totems usually belonged to a whole village. A wife who was from another village would never reveal her totem to her husband. The African believed that his totem possessed half of his soul. Some even believed that one could turn into his totem to seek vengeance upon an enemy.

It is clear then that totems played an important part in the folktales of Africa. There was little in African life or culture which totems did not greatly influence.

Elephant mask
from Baudjoun,
Bamilike village
in Cameroon

# A TOTEM TALE AMONG THE THONGA TRIBE

When Titishane wed a man
    And left her parents' house,
Her parents wisely counseled her,
    But did not tell her spouse.

An elephant they told her take.
    It was their family totem.
But she would have no part of it,
    And thought that totem hokum.

"Then take an antelope along,
    We also hold it dear."
But Titishane boldly said:
    "I won't, but have no fear."

"Instead of these, I'll take your cat."
    But they opposed her whim.
Since it was totem of their tribe,
    They would not part with him.

# A Tale Among the Thonga Tribe

The heartless daughter brashly said:
    "I've got to have that cat.
If you love me, then you will see
    That cat is where I'm at."

So parents parted with their cat,
    Chief totem of their clan.
Then Titishane took it home,
    But didn't tell her man.

She hid the cat at home each night,
    But took it with her daily.
And as she hoed her garden plot,
    The cat would dance quite gaily.

Some children heard the goings on.
    Her husband they informed.
He hid and watched the cat's routine,
    And then he really stormed.

He killed the cat and as it died,
    Dear Titishane fainted.
If husband had not acted soon,
    His wife might well be sainted.

She told him he must wrap the corpse
 And put it in a mat,
For she herself would surely die,
 If she looked at the cat.

She took it to her folks who said:
 "We cat clan are undone."
And as the village peered at it,
 All perished one by one.

The husband saw this gruesome sight,
 And left with dead unburied.
He hurried back to find a wife,
 For now he was unmarried.

Sometimes when totems of a clan,
 Die from the hunter's spear,
That clan will vanish from the earth,
 And never reappear.

We all have totems in our life,
 And superstitious fear.
At times we will deny that fact
 But then we're insincere.

# A Tale Among the Thonga Tribe

The idiosyncrasies we have,
  Are totems we've concealed.
We've placed them in forgotten tombs
  To hide the things we feel.

But sometimes they escape these tombs,
  And set for us new rules.
When they invade our consciousness,
  We act like witless fools.

Don't let your life be guided by
  Some fear or former problem.
It's reason that must rule your life
  And not some whacky goblin.

# ANIMAL TALES

There are a great number of animal stories in African folktales. Bantu lore is replete with tales of animals, birds, and insects of every sort. Many stories deal with the origins of entities and why things are as they are: why snakes have no legs, why the hare has a short tail, why the parrot has bright tail feathers, why the spider has a flattened body and lives in the dark. Africans were so familiar with animals that they just took them for granted. Since animals were a part of life, they wanted to know all they could about them. For this reason, animals became part and parcel of their folktales.

Africans loved a sense of fair play which is constantly brought out in stories where the weak confound the mighty. They treasured the superiority of brain power over physical strength. By brain power they meant a wiliness or cunning more than a greatness of mind. In these fairytales, which were the Africans' playground for a kind of irresponsible fancy, we must not only look for entertainment but we must look for the conveyance of ethical ideals.

Certain animals were more cunning than others: the jackal, hare, spider, chameleon and crocodile. These were the victors. The victims were the lion, elephant, hippopotamus, rhinoceros and the leopard.

# WHY SNAKES HAVE NO LEGS

There was a time when snakes had legs
    And millipedes had eyes.
But this no longer is the case,
    As folklore verifies.

A millipede was happily
    Invited to a dance.
It borrowed legs from friendly snake,
    Its dancing to enhance.

The snake agreed, but in return
    Asked from the millipede
To use its shrewd, discerning eyes,
    So it could better read.

So each exchanged what had been asked,
    As friendship did compel.
The millipede could dance all night.
    The snake could read quite well.

The snake exchanged its legs for eyes
    Which millipede forsook.
So while all legs were at the dance,
    All eyes were in a book.

# Why Snakes Have No Legs

The millipede called on the snake
    That night when dance had ended.
It wanted back those missing eyes
    The serpent had befriended.

The snake would not return the eyes,
    And this was indiscreet.
For then the little millipede
    Would not give back the feet.

This is the way that things still stand,
    In spite of how each begs,
The millipede without its eyes,
    The snake without its legs.

"To cut off nose to spite one's face!"
    All sages think is folly.
But losing legs for extra eyes!
    Is truly melancholy.

The serpent was the victim of
    The greed of its desire.
Without its legs it only crawls
    And slithers through the mire.

It could have walked with head in clouds,
    Instead of in the weeds,
If it had given back the eyes
    Of dancing millipede.

No one's enriched by what he steals.
    The thief makes himself poor.
For feelings of his guilt and greed
    He cannot long endure.

# WHY BIRDS ARE MULTICOLORED

In the beginning birds were white,
    But they thought this quite dull.
For how on earth could people tell
    A parrot from a gull.

They asked their God, Mulungo,
    To paint them like the flowers.
They said: "Be sure to use a paint
    That won't wash off in showers."

Mulungo ordered all the birds
    To fly before his throne.
The pots of paint were sitting there,
    Some bright, some dull in tone.

He took his brush to paint each bird.
    He called them one by one.
Each bird lined up to take its turn,
    Until the job was done.

The Che Mlanda was a bird
    That loved to agitate.
But every time he chirped, "Me next."
    Mulungo bid him wait.

# The Wisdom of African Mythology

The artist painted brilliantly.
    The plumage was exquisite.
It seemed that he outdid himself
    Each time a bird would visit.

The Che Mlanda chirped and chirped,
    Becoming quite a pest.
Mulungo called him out of turn
    Before he did the rest.

He dipped his brush into the paint
    And painted him dull brown.
And so that bird's the only one
    That doesn't have renown.

All other birds in Africa,
    Are known for brilliant hues.
But this dull bird's the only bird
    You'll never find in zoos.

It got in trouble by its mouth,
    As we so often do.
Instead of taking things in stride,
    It acted like a shrew.

So learn the lesson this bird taught,
    And learn it right away.
Your mouth can cause you lots of grief
    And lead you far astray.

The one who really wants to be
    The standout in the crowd,
Is usually the dullest one,
    And also the most loud.

# LITTLE PEOPLE

Little people play an important role in the various mythologies of the world. There are the Leprechauns in Celtic Mythology and the cave dwelling dwarfs in Nordic Mythology. There are certain things, however, that are common everywhere to the little people of mythological literature. They are usually sensitive to their size. They often live in caves. They are skilled in certain arts, especially metal work. These very same facts are verified in African Mythology. Since dwarfs are found in Africa, one expects to find them in African Mythology.

The Swahili called these legendary dwarfs, Wabilikomo. They were twice the distance from one's middle finger to one's elbow. The Howe were little people in Yao Folklore. They made bitter everything they touched. If they ran through your garden, their little feet made vegetables rot. The Abatwa are much smaller than all other small people. They walk under the grass and sleep in ant hills. They have no villages but live among the rocks.

Dwarfs were usually contentious. They were envious of others because of their height. Among the various African tribes all dwarfs asked the same question when met by strangers: "When did you see me?" If it were from afar, then the stranger acknowledged dwarfs were somewhat tall. But if one did not see them until he was on top of them, they were angry, insulted, and would often kill the intruder. A person shot with one of the dwarf's arrows could never see who shot him, for it came from under the grass.

Among the Bushmen dwarfs, some were gentle, but others waged war on every living thing. The Abatwa were Bushmen. In some parts of Africa this name is applied to Pygmies. The Pygmies of Urundi considered themselves the true aborigines of the country. They were smiths and potters, hunters and nomads. They were mostly timid, but cruel and irascible. They were so shy that they dug tunnels underground to avoid meeting people. Pygmies were very black, lean and hairy. Their countrymen hated them and considered them animals. They were put down as subhuman because their life was so bare of material sophistication. African cosmologies simply say of them: "They have come otherwise." Some say they came from the cracks of trees in the time of Woto, the fourth chief of the Bushgongo. When embarrassed by his family, Woto retired to the forest where, in his loneliness, he uttered incantations. The trees opened and little men came forth. These were the Pygmies. They were regarded with terror and other tribes would never intermarry with them.

# THE POOR MKONYINGO

Mkonyingos were a pygmy tribe.
    Their bodies were quite small.
But worse, they had misshapen heads
    Much like a basketball.

They lived in caves at mountain tops,
    Where they were hardly known.
If someone came, they ran so fast,
    You'd think they were full-grown.

They were most shy and timid men,
    No larger than a child.
But when you saw their ugly heads,
    You knew they must be wild.

Their head size made things difficult,
    At night it made them weep.
They can't lay down, they must sit up,
    If they intend to sleep.

Top heavy heads are troublesome,
    When it is time for bed.
If one lays down, he can't get up,
    He cannot move his head.

So they sleep sitting by a wall.
  When rising, it assists them.
But if they fall throughout the day,
  They lay there 'til friends miss them.

They carry horns about their belts,
  To blow when they're in need.
They hope someone will pick them up,
  Before they go to seed.

It's fortunate there is no ice
  On streets where these guys live.
Although it would add humor to
  This little narrative.

They'd all be laying on their backs,
  And blasting on their horns.
Just waiting for the ice to melt
  All looking quite forlorn.

So much of life is lived like that,
  Frustrations all around.
Just when we think we have stood up,
  We're face down on the ground.

We need a sense of humor then
  In order to survive.
Unless it were in constant use,
  We'd hardly seem alive.

That's how the Africans endured,
  Through slavery and its ills.
Their wit and sense of humor were
  More valuable than pills.

African tribal society was divided into clans. Clans were the major subdivisions of the tribe. Some tribes had over a hundred clans, and some clans had over a thousand people. The clan was further divided into gates which were made up of a number of similar families. When a gate reached a certain size, it became a clan. Members of a clan assisted each other in time of need, especially in time of war.

The family included far more than just members of a household. A family included its ancestors both living and dead. It included all the wives, children, grandparents, aunts, uncles and cousins. It was the sum of all those who had common ancestors. Families themselves were divided into households, while each household was further divided into the individual members. Compounds of related families formed a village. The houses were round and faced the center of the compound.

African society focused on the family. The individual was but part of a whole. He did not and could not exist apart from the community. Nothing was more important than the family. It was through the family that one obtained offspring, and it was through offspring that one obtained the gift of immortality and reached the blissful state of the living-dead. This immortality was achieved only by continued remembrance in the minds of one's own descendants. As long as a person was remembered, he was preserved in a state of personal immortality. If parents had no children to remember them when they were physically dead, they vanished from existence.

Since the family was such an important part of African life, marriage was the duty of all Africans. It was a requirement of society itself. Those who did not marry were considered a curse upon their community. The unmarried man was a rebel, a law breaker. He was looked upon as abnormal. Since the unmarried rejected society, society must also reject the unmarried.

The choice of a mate was important in African life. Various tribes had various customs for choosing mates. Often times the choice was made by parents sometimes, even before birth. When the choice was made by the young people themselves, parents were closely consulted and their advice was followed, for marriage was considered an integral part of the corporate community. Marriage was a religious duty.

Clans were exogamous. Marriage among members of the same clan was forbidden. Africans believed the living-dead were displeased with marriages of close relatives. Since marriage was an expansion of society itself, society regulated marriages and celebrated the marriage ceremony with considerable festivity. Gatherings and parties, dancing and drinking, feasts and covenant making festivals, the exchange of gifts between families, ritual washings and fertility rites, all played a part in African marriages.

Procreation completed marriage. By birth one captured immortality as parents were perpetuated in their offspring. Those who died without children became forever dead. But as long as a person was remembered by heirs, he or she was in someway living. This concept of living-dead explains many marriage customs in Africa and why the Africans' social status was increased by the number of wives he had. If a man had no children, or only girls, he sought another wife to produce sons to survive him and keep him immortal. Polygamy was commonly practiced for it increased the possibility of, and the number of offspring, and in this way guaranteed immortality.

The only moral law or sanction regulating marriage and the family was the approval of the community. Morality consisted, not only in not breaking the communion of the living, the dead, and the spirits in god, but in maintaining it through charity. Those who broke this mystical link were punished by exclusion from the community which was the worst kind of punishment; for to be forgotten by family, puts one in a state of nonexistence.

Life after death was the bedrock of African theological thought. Ancestral spirits living in the memories of their offspring lived underground much like they lived on earth. They had their own chiefs and tribal assemblies. They continued to live a life not too different from their prior existence on earth. They received offerings and libations not because they needed them, but because they were symbols of love and signs that they had not been forgotten by their descendants. As long as the deceased African was remembered by those who loved him in life, he continued to live in some way and entered into that mystical life known as the living-dead.

Since the community was all-important to African society, physical birth into it was not sufficient. There must also be a ritual birth or an initiation into it. Through this initiation the individual was incorporated into the community and became conscious of his worth, his being, and the duties he had as a member of that community. Through these initiation rites the "I" and the "We" were identified. Every birth was like the arrival of spring. The child born was not just born into a family; he or she was born into a community. The offspring was not referred to as "my child," but rather "our" child.

A woman in Africa occupied a place of honor and prominence, a role that has been greatly reduced by European influence. She was the source of life's force and the guardian of the house. She was the depositor of a clan's past and the guarantor of its future. A person belonged to the family of the mother. A child's first name was followed by that of his mother. It was the mother who raised the child in an atmosphere of love, tenderness and freedom. It was she who perpetuated the community and was thereby esteemed by it. She needed no other task or interest to be fulfilled. Polygamy, however, had some built-in problems like the jealous co-wife and the cruel stepmother.

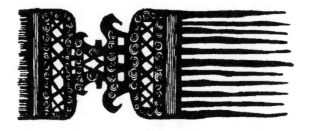

Some white men raised their eyebrows
    At the African's decorum,
For when it came to lovely wives,
    He always had a quorum.

Those whites looked down on practices
    They did not understand,
And thought because they're different,
    They must be contraband.

A marriage was the heart and soul
    Of tribal family life.
For man to reach the living-dead
    He had to have a wife.

A wife was needed to give birth
    To offspring so desired.
Unless man lived in memories,
    At death that man expired.

Each offspring was a precious gift,
    That only wives could give.
The more man's kids remembered him,
    The more in death he'd live.

Since children were so valuable,
    The more wives wed, the better.
For every single one of them
    Could be a child begetter.

If one wife were infertile,
    Another could give birth.
Or if one died, another loved
    The children she left on earth.

In times of trial or ill health,
    Another's hand was there.
If mothers would be indisposed,
    Another's love would care.

Of course there could be problems, too,
    Like jealousy and hate.
And all those petty little things
    That often complicate.

And built-in problems would occur
    That surely would cause strife.
But all in all things worked out well
    For each and every wife.

I think it's been a blessing though
    Monogamy was taught.
By Christian missionaries and
    The loving faith they brought.

But when we look upon the past
    Through past eyes we must see.
To judge the past by present norms,
    Denies a history.

# THE ORIGINS OF POLYANDRY AND POLYGAMY

Mount Kenya is God's resting place.
    It's there on earth he stays.
That's why a man will face its heights,
    When piously he prays.

Kikuyu, Masai, and Kamba,
    Each was God's noble son.
And each begot a royal tribe,
    That's never been outdone.

God showed his sons three instruments,
    An arrow, spear, and hoe.
He said each one must make a choice
    On how his race would go.

Masai, who chose the shepherd's spear,
    Was sent to tend great herds.
But Kamba chose the hunter's bow,
    And now kills beasts and birds.

Kikuyu chose the digging tool.
   His people till the land.
The nations that these sons begot
   Took traits from founder's hand.

So everything was going well
   Within their tribal life.
And everyone was most content,
   'Til Kikuyu took a wife.

Kikuyu married Moombi,
   Who bore him nine bright girls.
Kikuyu loved each one of them.
   All were his priceless pearls.

But he was sad he had no sons,
   And went aside to pray.
He journeyed to Mount Kenya, where,
   His father was that day.

There nine men suddenly appeared,
   A miracle, indeed.
He offered them his daughters' hands,
   If certain terms they'd heed.

# The Origins of Polyandry and Polygamy

The terms were matriarchal ties,
   To which they must agree.
Descent and all heredity
   Must by the mother be.

The men agreed and married them.
   They all lived as one clan,
A clan that bore the "Moombi" name,
   According to God's plan.

Then finally as the numbers grew,
   Each daughter gave her name
To her own individual clan,
   Which brought her lots of fame.

So Moombi's tribe had nine great clans,
   Named after each offspring,
All matriarchal kingdoms,
   Where women pulled the string.

Here polyandry was the rule
   That Moombi women set.
Each had as many husbands as
   She boastfully could get.

Men were mistreated and disgraced,
A cause for great alarm.
Since wives were stronger than their men,
The men must use their charm.

Each buttered up his wrathful spouse,
And soon was reconciled.
Each then made love and soon each wife
Was found to be with child.

When wives grew large and very weak,
The husbands then rebelled.
They set aside past practices,
And polyandry quelled.

Polygamy was introduced,
As men took many wives.
They changed the "Moombi" tribal name,
These men had long despised.

They called themselves Kikuyu tribes,
Named after their forefather.
They wished to change the names of clans,
But found it too much bother.

# The Origins of Polyandry and Polygamy

For women warned them bitterly
    What tactics they'd pursue.
If women clan names were replaced,
    Here's what each wife would do.

She'd put to death each new born boy,
    'Til men would ceased to be.
So men gave up the fight and said,
    The female names could be.

Polygamists soon quickly learned
    Two wives were not ideal.
For jealousies would surely grow,
    Which neither could conceal.

So one or many wives became
    The norm which men pursue.
For if a man had many wives,
    No one could pull a coup.

The man somehow still thinks he's boss,
    And women slyly let him.
And then with all their wily charms,
    Connive how they will get him.

But that, perhaps, by providence,
    Is woman's sacred role.
If love is to pervade the home,
    She must be in control.

A woman has been duly blessed,
    By powers from above,
To teach all those within her home,
    Just what it is to love.

A woman makes the family.
    The family makes the home.
The home when filled with motherhood
    Is like a metronome.

It measures every beat of love
    That builds the child's tomorrows.
It welcomes joys within the home,
    And turns away the sorrows.

It guarantees stability
    And pledges future life.
Where mothers will be models when,
    It's time to pick a wife.

# THE TWO HUMPS OF LAND
## OFF CAPE VERDE

A man named Momar had two wives,
    A Khary and a Koumba.
And each wife was as opposite
    As waltzes are from rumbas.

The first wife, Khary, was hunchbacked.
    And what a disposition!
Perhaps her dreadful grouchiness
    Was caused by her condition.

The other wife, named Koumba,
    Was loveable and sweet.
When she tried pleasing Khary, though,
    She only met defeat.

The more she tried to help with chores
    That Khary had to do,
The more she was insulted by
    That very ugly shrew.

She carried Momar's meals with love
    Into the field each day.
They ate beneath a tamarind,
    And laughed their cares away.

One day beneath that tamarind,
    A voice called Momar's wife.
It spoke to Koumba asking her,
    If peace had blessed her life?

Koumba, you see, was hunchbacked, too,
    But not the least bit bitter.
She lived her life without complaint,
    A doer, not a quitter.

She told the voice she was at peace,
    And knew her life was blessed.
The spirits knew this gentle soul
    In no way could protest.

The voice came from the spirit world
    That spoke to her that day,
Requesting that she listen well
    To what it had to say.

# The Two Humps of Land Off Cape Verde

"Beneath the full moon Friday night
　　Attend our spirit dance.
There will be someone next to you,
　　Who won't be there by chance."

"Say: `Hold the baby on my back,
　　For it's my turn to dance.'"
So Koumba did as she was told
　　And danced like in a trance.

When she got home her hump was gone.
　　So everyone rejoiced.
But Khary flew into a rage,
　　With anger loudly voiced.

Young Koumba then advised the shrew,
　　And told her what to do.
She must attend the spirit dance,
　　Next time full moon's in view.

And this is just what Khary did.
　　She knew what words to speak.
She memorized what she should say
　　To alter her physique.

"While I dance, hold my child," she said.
    "At once without delay."
But she who stood there next to her,
    Declined with this to say.

"Someone pulled that on me last month,
    But since has not returned.
I'll not be stuck like that again,
    For since then I have learned."

The spirit then stuck Koumba's hump
    Upon the back of Khary.
Instead of one hump there were two
    That she now had to carry.

She ran and jumped into the sea
    To drown her new found ills.
The sea refused to swallow her
    And left her humps as hills.

They're seen now off Cape Verde's shores,
    As Africa's last land.
Those two large humps from Khary's back
    That her pride could not stand.

# The Two Humps of Land Off Cape Verde

There are some lessons in this tale,
    And surely we should share them.
It's not the crosses that we have,
    It's rather how we bear them.

Both wives had problems to endure
    Of similar proportion.
One had an ugly attitude,
    And emphasized distortion.

The other found existing joys
    Amid life's many pains.
She didn't stress life's losses,
    She rather stressed its gains.

Her thoughts, which were so positive,
    Diminished her affliction.
Some say it was the spirit's work,
    But that is only fiction.

And now the rest is up to you.
    You'll be the way you think.
If positive, you'll cross wide seas.
    If negative you'll sink.

# INTERMEDIARY SPIRITS
## AND LESSER GODS

The notion of intermediary spirits was wide-spread among Africans. It was a common belief that man could not approach God alone or directly. It was universally understood man should approach God through a special person. Africans did not believe that these intermediaries blocked their way to God, but rather formed a bridge. Religion was not or could not be a private affair among Africans.

Not only was this notion of intermediaries between God and man held everywhere among Africans, but the intermediaries themselves were everywhere the same. First of all, there were the priests who were formally trained and commissioned. They could be male or female. The office was handed on mostly by inheritance or appointment. The priestly office was engaged in private as well as public rites.

Next, there were oracles known as prophets and seers. They were usually elders who gave ritual advice and were considered mouthpieces for various divinities. Thirdly, there were medicinemen who counteracted the effects of evil magic by their knowledge and mystical powers. By those same powers, they exercised a beneficial magic on behalf of the community. Fourthly, there were rainmakers, who offered prayers and sacrifices to God begging for rain, the most valuable commodity in a hot and arid climate. Fifthly, there were kings or tribal chiefs.

Since kings were considered chosen by God, proper conduct was demanded of them. If God became angry with leaders, the whole nation was punished by drought, locusts, or floods. Sixthly there were the elders who assisted priests or performed sacrificial rites when priests were absent. Next, there was the whole realm of the living-dead. These intermediaries were the largest group who brought prayers and offerings to God. Sometimes they brought messages back from him. Eighthly, the belief in special spirits created by God to act as His intermediaries existed. And lastly, in some tribes, certain animals were regarded as intermediaries between man and God. The Sidamo considered hyenas and serpents as such.

Africans worshipped God any time and any place. There were no general rules; and individual rules might differ from place to place. Many tribes prayed daily. Most tribes had sacred rituals at birth, puberty and before marriage. There were rituals for planting and harvesting. Africans turned to God anytime the need arose. When they did, it was usually one of the intermediaries that kept the individual in liturgical contact with the spirit world.

Most tribes had sacred shrines. Seventeen thousand divinities had shrines among the Yorubas. A shrine was considered the Divinity's face and made him present in a special way. There was no limit to where or when Africans performed acts of worship. They were a deeply religious people and attributed religious meaning to the whole of existence.

# GOD'S FIRST CONTACT WITH MAN

Mulunga was the Yao's God.
    And here he made his berth.
He then created every beast,
    That lived upon this earth.

The beasts were his aesthetic work.
    He loved them very much.
And each reflected brilliantly
    Their god's artistic touch.

A calm and joy then filled the earth,
    And peace reigned everywhere,
Until strange creatures fell into
    A bold chameleon's snare.

A man and wife they claimed to be,
    But such things were unknown.
All beasts were puzzled when they saw
    Them at Mulunga's throne.

Mulunga, too, was troubled by
    These things he didn't know.
He placed them in his royal fields,
    Where they could feed and grow.

One day they killed a buffalo
    And built the world's first fire.
Mulunga fled its roaring flames,
    Believing he'd expire.

He climbed a spider's flimsy web
    Up high into the sky.
And there declared this punishment
    When these strange creatures die.

They'll come before Mulunga's throne,
    And serve him as his slaves,
For slaughtering his animals,
    And multiplying graves.

But animals shall stay on earth,
    And sleep in peaceful rest.
While man at death must go to God
    As his unwelcome guest.

Mulunga was a bit confused,
    So things got out of hand.
Man wasn't made for animals,
    But animals for man.

# God's First Contact with Man

Some do not understand this truth,
 And so will not eat meat.
They speak of those who wear fine furs,
 With words I can't repeat.

They think it is an evil deed
 To eat fine steaks and chops.
The only thing they'll let you eat,
 Are things that grow as crops.

But soon they'll probably talk about
 The vegetables' rights.
And then they'll ban all fruits and nuts
 From human appetites.

The African's too sensible
 For sentimental highs.
He knows the risks of rattlesnakes
 And ugly tsetse flies.

Mulunga might have made all beasts,
 But sane men surely know.
To squash a mean mosquito bug
 Is still quite apropos.

# The Wisdom of African Mythology

I'm sure Mulunga quickly learned
    This all important fact.
And those who still deny this truth,
    Are putting on an act.

The Africans were sure of this,
    For beasts served them so well,
As food to eat and skins to roof
    The huts in which they dwell.

And they were not afraid to eat
    A caribou or cow,
Nor thought they'd ill-treat oxen, if
    They made them pull a plough.

The Africans were just too smart
    To speak of insect rights,
Or rights of creepy, crawling things,
    Or grubby parasites.

Such talk is utter nonsense, then,
    Where animals abound,
Where snakes or scorpions end up
    Sometimes in one's compound.

If you don't take that serpent's life,
 It surely could take yours.
So kill the threat before it strikes,
 Then eat it as hors d'oeuvres.

And if do-gooders preach to you
 About that viper's rights,
Take them to a mosquito nest,
 And watch them scratch their bites.

And when they swat those awful bugs,
 Their lives become a lie.
For all those rights they preached about
 Have somehow gone awry.

# OL-OKUM, A LESSER GOD

Ol-Okum was a lesser god.
    He lived beneath the sea,
He thought he rivaled God himself,
    And wanted all to see.

His kingdoms were the seven seas.
    He rode upon their waves.
He thought himself all-powerful,
    For fishes were his slaves.

To prove himself God's equal, he
    Decided on a test.
He'd let his many followers
    Judge which of them was best.

He challenged God to richly dress,
    And he would do the same.
And he who dressed more brilliantly,
    Was winner by acclaim.

When came that day agreed upon,
    God's envoy was dispatched,
The versatile chameleon,
    That anything could match.

# Ol-Okum, a Lesser God

Ol-Okum came in finest dress,
    Ascending from the deep.
God's messenger was dressed the same,
    Which made Ol-Okum weep.

Ol-Okum then excused himself,
    And went back to the sea.
He added rich and costly things,
    His finest jewelry.

With confidence he came back up.
    In splendor he was clad,
But saw chameleon, too, had changed,
    Exactly as he had.

Each time Ol-Okum went below,
    He'd rise again with shame.
For every time he changed his clothes,
    God's envoy dressed the same.

Ol-Okum knew he'd lost the test,
    Before the test began.
If he could not outshine God's page,
    He'd be an also-ran.

So he called off the test proposed,
    And went back to the sea.
Not knowing God outsmarted him
    By skilled chicanery.

Since then Ol-Okum's satisfied
    To stay in second place.
The sea remains within its bounds.
    It wants no more disgrace.

Some blacks might think they have a place,
    In which they must remain.
Such thoughts are utter nonsense, though,
    And only cause them pain.

They're not competing with some God,
    As proud Ol-Okum was.
They must deal with equality,
    As everybody does.

We're all on life's big carousel,
    And reach for rings of gold.
No matter what our backgrounds are
    No man is in a mold.

Blacks do have disadvantages,
   In our society.
But that must never hold them back,
   Or humbled make them be.

They can excel in everything,
   As they have often done.
And when it comes to placing first,
   They've only just begun.

Ol-Okum, then, must never be
   A model for the black.
He quit when things got difficult.
   That's when he should attack.

# MEDICINE MEN

Medicine men were treasured as
   Great specialists in magic.
Through charms and incantations then,
   They'd ward off all things tragic.

They were a part of village life,
   With blessings and with curse.
The people knew without their skills,
   The bad would get much worse.

And so these men were called upon
   To frustrate witches' plans.
They'd strike at graves of witchcraft deaths
   To thwart their talismans.

Then animals would rise from graves,
   The spirits of the dead,
And saunter off to witch's home,
   To which the witch had fled.

As witch's family killed each beast,
   A family member died,
In vengeance for the witch's deed,
   As folk myths certified.

Until the family of the witch
    Paid cattle as a fee,
Paid to the family of the dead,
    From curse they'd not be free.

Belief and magic clearly merged
    As God did things through men.
In Africa two worlds were one,
    The "voodoo" and "amen."

The world of magic was two-fold,
    The evil and the good.
The evil used it evilly,
    But good men never would.

It was the belief in Africa
    That nothing's accidental.
Disease and common tragedies
    Are not coincidental.

The sorcerer's behind these things
    With magical attack.
What he will do to images,
    Will soon be done in fact.

That's why they hated sorcery,
    And why they had such fear,
Of evil eyes and magic snakes
    That ended one's career.

The way to counteract witchcraft
    Was by a medicine man.
The force of God was used by him
    To frustrate witchcraft's plan.

We sometimes think these Africans
    Were steeped in superstition,
That they have not advanced too much
    Since days of abolition.

But others are the ones enslaved
    By foibles they deny.
They think because they're lily white
    They have an alibi.

But as the whites drift from God's truths
    That He's revealed to us,
They grow more superstitious than
    Some wizard's syllabus.

For who is it that lives by stars,
    Or horoscopic bunk?
And who supports astrologers,
    Or buys their published junk?

And who supports the fortune teller?
    The black man who is poor?
And when it comes to Ouija boards,
    Who is the connoisseur?

It is the white, who's bored with life,
    And lives without a goal.
It's not the black man seeking God,
    In his religious soul.

# THE LESSER GOD ESHU

Yoruba's mediator was
    A spirit known as Eshu.
He was a very angry God
    As everyone alive knew.

This Eshu was most powerful
    Of all the lesser Gods.
And only he, the God supreme,
    Could ride on him slip-shod.

And this he often had to do
    To keep this God in check.
For he was never satisfied,
    Unless a life he'd wreck.

Confusion was his great delight.
    On that he really thrived.
Sharp discord he would introduce,
    Wherever he arrived.

One time he saw a peaceful home,
    In which there were two wives.
He instantly sought to destroy
    The peace that filled their lives.

# The Lesser God Eshu

He gave a lovely headdress to
    One of the man's two wives.
The other fumed with jealousy,
    As Eshu had devised.

He would not cease 'til turmoil reigned,
    For strife was his first love.
He fed the warring falcon,
    But starved the peaceful dove.

I think that every club or group
    Has Eshu in disguise,
The hostile, vicious malcontent,
    That must antagonize.

He's not at ease where concord reigns,
    Or where friendships can bloom.
He's sad unless turmoil appears,
    And lives are filled with gloom.

And racial tensions are his thing,
    As Eshu's thing was wives.
He gets his kicks from racial hate,
    That he instills in lives.

So do not be a victim of
    His bigotry and hate.
And know that he has conquered that
    Which he can alienate.

He's but a witless imbecile,
    We pity more than scorn.
He seems to lack the decency
    With which most men are born.

# THE SUN AND MOON AND EARTH

The sun does not play a prominent role in African mythology nor in African religious worship. It was always present, sending down its rays of scorching heat. There was no need to call it back from a winter's absence by offering sacrifices as was done in northern climates. It was considered more important to offer sacrifices to the rain-god, for rain was the more needed commodity.

The Ashanti tribe knew the sun as Nyankopan, or Lisa, the king of the universe. The moon was his queen. Mawu, the moon, was kind. Lisa, the sun, was fierce and harsh. Mawu was older. She was a woman and a mother and was gentle and refreshing. Throughout the day men suffered under Lisa's heat, but at night in the cool moonlight they danced and told stories. Coolness was a sign of wisdom. So Mawu was looked upon as the wisdom of the world. Lisa was its strength.

The Krachi tribe of Togo believed the sun married the moon and gave birth to the many stars. The moon soon tired of her spouse and took a lover. The sun then put her out and divided their children and possessions. At times, the children who remained with the sun, fought with the children who went off with the moon. These fights are called storms. The moon doesn't want her children to fight, so she waves a flag of peace, a cloth of many colors. Men call it the rainbow. If the moon invades the territory of the sun, the sun tries to eat her. This is an eclipse.

Among the Dagomba people it was thought the sun kept a ram that caused thunder when it stamped its feet. It caused lightning when it shook its tail. Rain was its hair falling from its tail. When it rushed about the face of the moon, it caused wind.

There are many folktales like this about the sun and the moon to explain causality. Cape Bushmen speak of a young man who wept at his mother's death. The moon appeared and told him not to weep, for his mother was only sleeping as the moon does. The moon seems to die but always returns to life. The young man would not believe the moon and insisted she was deceiving him. This accusation angered the moon. She struck the youth, split his lip, and changed him into a hare. That's why hares have a cleft lip. She then cursed the hare and said it would be hunted by dogs forever, caught, and torn to pieces.

In Angola it was believed a son of the first man refused to marry one of his own people. He preferred to marry a daughter of the sun and moon. He sought a messenger to bring his request to heaven. Animals and birds refused to go. Finally the frog said he would go. The frog knew the daughters came down a spider's web to draw water from the earth. He jumped into one of their jars and was soon carried to the sun. The frog hid in the girl's room, cast a spell on her, and stole both her eyes. The next morning the sun discovered this deed and asked a diviner what was wrong with his lovely daughter. The diviner informed the sun that the girl's lover had cast a spell on her and she would surely die if she were not sent to him. So the sun ordered the spider to weave a web and take his daughter down to earth to her lover. The frog went on ahead and when the girl arrived, he restored her eyes and brought her to the boy. They were married and lived happily ever after. She never returned to heaven, but the frog often goes back and forth. He sometimes falls in rainstorms.

The Luyia people of Kenya have a belief similar to the biblical account of Jacob and his brother Esau. When God first created the moon and the sun, the moon was brighter and bigger and the older of the two brothers. The envious sun then attacked his brother. The sun was badly defeated and begged for mercy which his brother, the moon, granted. They fought another time and this time the sun threw the moon into the mud and splashed him with dirt so he was not as bright as he had been. Finally God intervened and declared the sun would now be brighter and shine in the day for workers and kings. The moon would shine at night for thieves and witches. God said the moon had been foolish when he granted mercy to the sun. The moon should have finished off his brother when he had the opportunity. By chicanery, the deceitful sun, the younger of the two, got the best of his older brother, the moon, and still retains the upperhand.

# IF YOU RIDE THE BULL, DON'T EAT IT

Young Murile's mother scolded him,
    And he began to pout.
He stole his father's magic stool,
    And angrily set out.

He told the stool to carry him
    As far as heaven's moon.
The magic stool obeyed his wish,
    And they arrived there soon.

He asked the moon's inhabitants
    To take him to their chief.
And what he saw when he arrived
    Was far beyond belief.

The chief and all his people there
    Ate all their food uncooked,
Their meat and all their vegetables,
    And fishes that they hooked.

Then Murile soon discovered that
    Moon people knew not fire.
He built a rather roaring one
    Which everyone admired.

He showed them how they too could make
    A fire just as good,
By taking dried grass in their hands,
    While rubbing hunks of wood.

They thought he was some foreign God,
    And heaped upon him gold.
Soon wives and children, herds and flocks,
    Made up his rich household.

But then in time he longed for home
    And past acquaintanceship.
He sent a mocking bird ahead
    To pre-announce his trip.

No one on earth would believe its tale,
    And so the bird returned.
But Murile did not believe the bird
    Had made the long sojourn.

So mocking bird flew back to earth
    And seized the father's cane,
To prove that he had carried out
    What had been foreordained.

# If You Ride the Bull, Don't Eat It

The lad with all his family, then,
    With herds and flocks complete,
Set out to travel to the earth
    Where land and sky both meet.

He asked a bull to carry him,
    And promised in return,
He'd never eat the flesh of bulls;
    Their meat he'd always spurn.

He rode the bull right to his house.
    His relatives rejoiced.
When asked for deference for the bull,
    They promised with one voice.

At last his father killed the bull,
    When it grew very old.
His mother melted down the fat,
    At least that's what I'm told.

She put some fat in Murile's food,
    Which he then quickly ate.
But as he did, the food cried out,
    It would retaliate.

Murile began to sink into
    The earth beneath his feet.
For promise made and then not kept,
    This was his balance sheet.

And as he sank into the earth,
    His mother sadly grieved him.
He asked her why she'd done this deed,
    And why she had deceived him?

And that's the way the story ends,
    With sadness and deception.
That many lives will end this way
    Is true without exception.

How many lives have since been wrecked
    By cunning and deceit.
Men try to play a masquerade
    With everyone they meet.

Their promises they do not keep,
    If keeping's difficult.
They choose the easy path through life,
    And outrages result.

## If You Ride the Bull, Don't Eat It

They step upon another's toes
    To further their own goals.
But just like Murile in the myth,
    They're digging their own holes.

They'll slowly sink into the ground,
    The ground we know as death.
And they will be quite terrified
    To breathe their final breath.

They'll think of what they really were,
    And what they could have been.
For few will have the chance to be
    A bull equestrienne.

Their life will pass by in review,
    Its sadness and its joys.
The things they thought important once,
    They'll find were only toys.

# RAIN AND RAINBOW SPIRITS

Those men who make the rain to fall,
    Or make the rain to cease,
Are those who know which clouds to call
    So rains they will release.

They're found throughout all Africa,
    And always charge a fee.
And if a drought has lasted long,
    The greater it will be.

But when it's time to stop the rain,
    A rainbow God will form.
Its light and colors fill the sky,
    Announcing end of storm.

And where that rainbow meets the earth
    Great treasures can be found.
A fierce ram guards that very spot,
    And dangers there abound.

The rainbow meant so many things
    To many different folks.
To some it meant God's blessings,
    To some, God's counter-strokes.

The Zulus thought the rainbow's arch
    Bedecked and crowned their queen.
Kikuyus thought it was a beast,
    Quite gross and serpentine.

The rain God Tsui'goab was
    Adored by Hottentots.
In taking oaths they called his name
    For blessings he begot.

And Deng was an important God
    Among the Dinga tribes.
Fierce lightning was the club he used,
    As we learn from their scribes.

The man killed by this mighty club
    Could not be rightly mourned.
For if a man offended God,
    He surely should be scorned.

Most men are chasing rainbows still,
    Though they don't understand.
They call them by fictitious names,
    As if they're contraband.

They're living in a world of dreams,
   And simply won't awake.
They have so long deceived themselves,
   To eat and keep their cake.

They soon must face reality,
   And wake up from those dreams.
And then they will discover that
   This world "ain't" what it seems.

# THAT'S A "CROC"

There was a Malagasy clan
    With a funny after-life.
Their mother once lived in a stream,
    As a crocodile's wife.

One day she got caught in a trap
    And married then a man.
She bore the man two healthy sons,
    Then back to river ran.

She went back to her crocodile,
    And there she has remained.
But both her sons lived on dry land,
    With families they had gained.

Among these sons' descendants though,
    The crocodile's tabooed.
For if they ate one, it could be
    Grandmother barbecued.

When members of this clan now die,
    Their body grows a tail.
And feet grow into ugly claws,
    While skin becomes all scale.

These dead turn into crocodiles,
    Then travel to a river,
To meet their ancient matriarch,
    Who hopes her sons forgive her.

You talk about weird hang-ups and
    Complexes that are strange.
Or playing cards without full decks,
    Or living life short-changed!

There are a lot of complexes.
    There's probably a zillion,
Electra and the Oedipus,
    And now the Crocodilian.

I understand Electra and
    The Oedipus complex.
But by the Crocodilian kind,
    I truly am perplexed.

If mama is a crocodile,
    And swims about in streams,
Her human kids must be confused,
    And have nightmarish dreams.

# That's A "Croc"

And talk about that goodnight kiss,
    From mama floating by.
They could end up inside her gut,
    If something's in her eye.

Or talk about abandoned kids,
    Or kids whom folks defile!
How do you tell a little child
    His mom's a crocodile?

When kids have some Electra traits,
    I easily understand.
The mother is at fault I'm sure,
    And needs a reprimand.

But what about those little tykes
    Whose mother thinks it stylish
To give her kids a tail and claws,
    To make them crocodilish.

I'm sure not many other kids
    Have complexes so great,
As those whose mothers have become
    A crocodile's mate.

There are a lot of mothers now
  Confused in raising kids.
So is it any wonder why
  Their children hit the skids?

It's not those kids who need our help.
  Their mothers are to blame.
Too bad their moms aren't crocodiles.
  And that's our culture's shame!

# THE GODDESS EARTH

All Africans believed there was
    A spiritual force,
That animated everything
    And was its power source.

They thought the earth prolific.
    She was the wife of God.
So nothing that the earth would do
    Was ever done slipshod.

The goddess earth was worshipped by
    All people everywhere.
Before they dug for salt or roots,
    They offered her a prayer.

Before a grave was ever dug,
    Libations sought permission.
The earth who was the Queen of death,
    Then welcomed grave's addition.

She was called Ala by most tribes,
    The world's most fertile source.
The mother of morality,
    And living things, of course.

# The Wisdom of African Mythology

Her spirit dwelled on mountain tops,
    'Specially Kilimanjaro.
Her powers and her taboos were
    The source of lots of sorrow.

Her spirit, too, filled lakes and streams,
    Which mortals knew as Zin.
If humans ever looked on them,
    Their mortal life would end.

The universe of Africans,
    Was filled with godlike signs.
And every nook and cranny there
    Had many sacred shrines.

Those Africans who came as slaves
    Brought their religious thought.
So that's why almost all of them
    Lived truly as they ought.

But when they learned the white man's ways,
    Some lives were rearranged.
And those who were thus victimized,
    Were dreadfully short-changed.

## PRIEST AND PRIESTESSES

It is unfortunate that non-Africans pin labels on Africans. The non-African does not understand the Africans' ancient beliefs. In his ignorance he brands those beliefs as superstitious, crude, and even childish. Africans attributed to their gods characteristics which were more or less human. Their gods offered them protection and in return they offered the gods respect. Religion was the regulating force in their lives. The pagan Africans lived in an age of faith. This faith gave meaning to their lives.

These pagan religions offered Africans a well-rounded system of moral and spiritual teaching. It was this teaching that enabled them to build and maintain a stable society of law and order. From their religions, they gleaned their ideas of good and evil, they comforted their sick and dying, and they gave meaning and goals to their difficult existence.

These goals were reached in a variety of ways by many different tribes. When groups splintered off from parent tribes as they searched for new lands, they often carried with them their old beliefs, but modified them as conditions warranted. Certainly those living in rain forests who seldom saw the sky had different views of the world than those who lived on grassy plains. Those living by the sea viewed life differently than those living in the vast interior.

No matter how varied were particular religious beliefs or practices, they all shared a common idea of the supernatural. These groups believed in a single supreme deity from whom all things came forth. This God was an energy or life giving force. The dead did not really die, but left the earth only to join this life force. The dead kept their spiritual identity and belonged to a vast community made up of the living, the dead, and those yet to be born.

The supreme God played little part in man's life; he intrusted that life and the administration of the universe to lesser Gods. Africans had no churches. Their temples were but wayside altars of wood or stone known as shrines. These shrines were sacred places where Africans came to consult oracles or to pray. The priest or priestesses, who were the custodians of these shrines, were people of notable importance and were usually skilled in physical or mental healing through psychological insights or herbal medicine. Power to mediate between the spirit world was attributed to them. Training for their many duties was long and arduous.

The priest or priestess was often sought to play the role of an oracle in an effort to solve problems or answer questions. Since pythons were considered sacred in Africa, the python priestess filled an important task in African religious life and is often referred to in African mythology. Snakes, too, are frequently mentioned in tales and myths of this country where snakes were so common.

# THE SERPENT OF WAGADU

The land of Ghana knew great wealth,
    In harvest and in gold.
The rains fell there abundantly,
    And mines gave multifold.

In Ghana people long believed
    Prosperity was due,
Not to their ingenuity,
    But to a snake they knew.

The serpent's name was Bida and
    It lived within a pit.
Each year a girl was sacrificed,
    The snake's prerequisite.

In time each tribe must take its turn
    To sacrifice a girl.
When came the tribe of Wagadu,
    The serpent won a pearl.

The victim's name was Sia,
    Fair child of Wagadu,
A very pretty maiden,
    Engaged to Amadou.

This Amadou, the silent one,
    Was saddened by the choice.
But when it came to tribal things,
    He simply had no voice.

But Amadou, the Taciturn,
    Would by his actions speak.
For with the serpent on that night,
    He would play hide-and-seek.

He honed his saber all day long,
    'Til it could cut the wind.
When darkness came upon the earth,
    With snake he would contend.

The tribal elders led the girl,
    As drums announced her fate.
She slowly walked up to the pit,
    Without an advocate.

The elders asked forgiveness then,
    And left the girl alone.
She covered eyes and knelt in prayer,
    But uttered not a moan.

Then Bida slithered from its hole,
  And deadly venom spit.
The serpent then crawled back again,
  Descending to its pit.

It reappeared and wrapped around
  The maid of Wagadu.
Then Amadou brought down his sword,
  And cut the snake in two.

Then instantly the monster grew
  Another frightful head.
So Amadou then struck again,
  To make sure it was dead.

And many times he swung his sword,
  Beheading snake each time.
But every time a head grew back,
  Like branches on a vine.

Then as the seventh head fell off,
  The snake was heard to say.
A curse will come upon this land,
  Beginning with this day.

## The Serpent of Wagadu

For seven years no rain will fall
    Upon the fields of Ghana.
No rains of water nor of gold
    Will bless this rich savanna.

Then as the monstrous serpent died,
    All rivers ceased to be.
The fields were barren without crops,
    As far as eyes could see.

No longer could men pan for gold,
    Nor find wealth in their mines.
Soon famine ravished everyone,
    And Ghana then declined.

So often we will play life's games,
    In order to succeed.
The values we once held so dear,
    We readily concede.

We'll sacrifice the things we love
    To get ahead in life.
We'll trade off children and our friends,
    We'll even trade our wife.

# The Wisdom of African Mythology

We're like the tribes of Wagadu,
    Who sacrificed their own.
And threw her to that ugly snake,
    To tear her skin from bone.

There are but few like Amadou,
    Who'll fight against the wrong,
Who'll wield a sword against their greed
    When opposition's strong.

For when they think they've met their task,
    And cut off greed's mean head,
Allurements of some other kind
    Develop in its stead.

Sometimes it takes the seventh try
    To slay an ugly vice.
The problem is so many quit,
    When they have tried but twice.

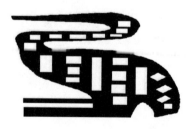

# FULANI WISDOM

Fulani tribes
    Might lie in words,
But never lie
    In wise proverbs.

The darkest night
    Will bring one fear.
But men bring more
    When they are near.

Fulanis like
    An elephant's meat!
It fills the pot,
    And cooks with heat.

To really know
    What's in the heart,
Just read the face;
    It is its chart.

Few men in time
    Get what's their due.
But when life ends
    They always do.

# A FULANI WARNING

There are six things
    That we must fear.
Most trouble comes
    When they are near.

The first thing is
    A ruling prince.
Against his greed,
    There's no defense.

The second is
    A running river.
It seldom is
    A kind forgiver.

The third thing is
    A hunter's knife.
Never trust it
    With your wife.

The fourth thing is
    A pretty maid.
She'll transport trouble
    And degrade.

The fifth thing is
    A piece of string.
I can't conceive
    What it will bring.

And darkness is
    The final thing.
Who knows what evils
    It will bring.

I'll bet you each
    Can add your own.
By now they should
    Be quite well known.

I'm sure most fears
    Are quite unfounded.
But on those fears
    Our lives are grounded

Each fear can keep
    Us from our duty,
As people think
    We're tutti-fruiti

Of all the fears,
    Upon our shelf.
We should fear most
    Our very self.

It was at Ife-Ife that
    God's children came to earth.
And where God's son Oduduwa,
    To humans first gave birth.

This site on earth was known to be
    The gods' most treasured spot.
Ogun had cleared it with an axe
    To be their Camelot.

The gods then chose him to be king,
    And offered him a crown.
But he who loved the hunter's life,
    Sought other hunting ground.

'Twas here that the Yoruba tribes
    Thought kingship was divine.
And asked Oduduwa, God's son,
    To be the king assigned.

At Ife-Ife culture thrived,
    And art and sculpture bloomed.
All nations throughout Africa
    Looked to it to be groomed.

Oranmiyan then came to rule,
 Oduduwa's young son.
A dynasty arose from him,
 That's never been outdone.

Its ruler was called "Alafin."
 Who was the country's king.
But council and prime minister
 Helped him in everything.

And if three times they said to him,
 "The gods and earth reject you."
The king must take his own life, then,
 And let the clan elect new.

So council would not interfere,
 Or special problems bring,
A council member had to die
 With the rejected king.

This kingdom was the rival of
 Great European courts,
As world renowned would travel there
 For cultural supports.

So when we call them primitives,
    We're simply out of touch.
We're ignorant of history
    And bigotry's our crutch.

We've never seen their priceless art,
    In ivory, bronze, and wood.
The bigot's mediocrity
    Has blinded us to good.

# THE DIVINE GIFT OF FOOD

According to the Ila Tribe,
    When God sent man to earth,
He gave man grain to be his food,
    But man knew not its worth.

Men sowed the grain and harvested
    Enormous crops of corn.
They ate as much as they could eat,
    Then burned the rest next morn.

A famine came. There was no food.
    The surplus had been burned.
But only after hunger pangs,
    Did men become concerned.

And so again they went to God,
    And asked for more fine grain.
God said they'd acted foolishly,
    And so should not complain.

Since they had burned his gift of grain,
    He'd give them only fruit.
This fruit and roots that they could dig
    Would be grain's substitute.

That's why since then most Africans
  Have lived on roots and fruit,
The grain once grown was wasted,
  Which left them destitute.

Some wasted it in brewing beer.
  Some burned it in the field.
Some ate so much they soon ran out,
  As greed went unrepealed.

And so it was that they returned
  To fruits and roots they'd dig.
The corn and grain they loved so much
  Gave way to yam and fig.

And still today this is the case.
  Extravagance prevails!
Man squanders that which he should save,
  And then he loudly wails.

Excessive waste and lavishness,
  Is sure a human trait.
What most men get, they want to spend,
  And they can hardly wait.

# The Divine Gift of Food

So corn and grain are symbols of
    Fine steaks and lobster tails,
Which men consume with finest wines,
    As foolishness prevails.

Then comes the day of reckoning,
    That rainy day we feared,
When nothing's left to pay our bills,
    For all has disappeared.

So back to figs and yams we go,
    The price of our fast living.
We all should live within our means,
    For debts are unforgiving.

Sometimes we should recork the wine,
    And drink Milwaukee beer.
And put aside the shrimp and steaks,
    And let hot dogs appear.

Few men have fiscal prudence, though,
    It's not our attribute.
We spend our dough like millionaires,
    And then eat yams and fruit.

# GRASSHOPPERS, RICE
# AND CRYING KIDS

One seldom would associate
　　Grasshoppers with fine rice.
But that's the way it really was,
　　If I might be precise.

There is a Malagasy tale
　　About just such a thing.
The facts I shall describe to you,
　　Astonishment will bring.

A child was playing by a stream.
　　Her mother worked nearby.
The child saw a grasshopper jump,
　　And sometimes it jumped high.

The young girl asked her mother if
　　She'd catch the bug for her.
She did and gave it to her child,
　　As if to reassure.

The bug in time then jumped away,
　　Perhaps, to find its bride.
And as it did the young girl sulked,
　　And then she loudly cried.

# Grasshoppers, Rice and Crying Kids

The mother searched but could not find
    The bug her daughter wanted.
The child got sick and then she died,
    The whole thing seemed quite haunted.

The mother wept such bitter tears,
    Her cries were heard by God,
Who told her to inter the child
    Beneath some marshy sod.

The mother sadly buried her
    In god's prescribed terrain.
And in a month a plant grew up
    Which bore a lovely grain.

God told the woman: "Pick the grain,
    Then pound it, and then cook it."
The grain had such a pleasant taste,
    That no one's since forsook it.

God told her she must name the grain
    After her daughter, Rice.
And that's what it has since been called,
    For she took God's advice.

# MORE ANIMAL TALES

The hare was the principal Bantu hero. It was a clever animal, depending on its speed and cunning to protect itself in open country. Since many southern blacks were descendants of the Bantu tribes, it is not surprising to see the hare of African folktales become the rabbit in Brer Rabbit of Black American literature and the hyena become Brer Fox, the hare's chief enemy. The hare was a common character in African folktales, as also was the spider, the tortoise and the jackal. The frog, chameleon, the crocodile, the python and the hyena were less frequently mentioned characters.

The hare became the jackal among Nama people. What Bantu tribes attributed to the hare, Hottentot folklore attributed to the jackal. The Bantu tribes considered the hare's habit of moving its mouth, as if talking to itself, a sign of its wisdom. The tortoise and the spider were often set against the hare as a match for his wits in an effort to develop a sense of fair play.

The following stories of the hare, the tortoise, and other animals will show us why Africans so loved their innumerable tales about the animals with which they shared the land. In these tales they attributed human feelings and desires to animals, and even drew ethical ideals from their behavior. They were in close contact with these animals, and asked endless questions concerning them: why the cock had fine feathers; why the ram pawed the ground when it thundered; why the goat was domesticated; why bats fly at night; why crocodiles did not die in water; why snakes shed their skins; why a parrot had a red tail; why the chameleon's head was so square; why mosquitoes endlessly bothered ears; why sparrows flew into smoke; why spiders became bald; why leopards had spots, and why hares had long ears. These wonderings are but a few of the questions posed and answered in the many interesting and delightful African folktales about animals of every sort.

The African lived his life close to the animals with which he shared the jungle. Therefore, it is not at all surprising animals played such a prominent role in the African's daily thoughts and conversation, and in his country's oral literature. Fortunately, this literature has been carefully preserved and handed down throughout the centuries so even to this day, all of us today can find such delight in its wit and charm.

# WHY LEOPARDS HAVE SPOTS

The Leopard in its jungle home
    Was friendly with Lord Fire.
So everyday he called upon
    The flame he so admired.

But not once did Lord Fire appear
    At leopard's humble den.
The leopard's wife then rashly thought
    That fire was not a friend.

The leopard begged Lord Fire to call,
    At least to please his spouse.
But Lord Fire said: "I never call
    Upon a friendly house."

"I'm not all that I seem to be.
    It's best I keep my space.
The only time I function well
    Is in a fire place."

When leopard pressed, Lord Fire said,
    He simply could not walk.
He needed roads of dried out leaves.
    To visit and to talk.

# Why Leopards Have Spots

He could not walk; he only crawled,
    But sometimes sped along,
If winds came up to help him out,
    And if those winds were strong.

The wife thought she would call his bluff.
    And gathered leaves galore.
She set them all about the road
    That led to her front door.

A wind came up; Lord Fire cracked;
    To leopard's house he sped.
As he approached his good friend's home,
    All things before him fled.

The house burst forth in blazing flames,
    As leopard's friend drew near.
His fingers touched the leopard's skin,
    And black spots then appeared.

Sometimes a friend can do us in,
    Without intending harm.
What's meant a friendly social call,
    Becomes a four-alarm.

When trouble seems to come our way,
    We often get excited.
And yet the trouble that invades,
    We often have invited.

We always want what we can't have,
    And search for it in vain.
We think it will bring happiness,
    But all it brings is pain.

We're like the foolish leopard's wife,
    Inviting trouble in.
We rashly act without forethought,
    Or mental discipline.

We form the road of leaves ourselves,
    That trouble travels on.
And then before we realize,
    The things we loved are gone.

We then have scars like leopard spots,
    That mark us as the fool.
The things that we should celebrate,
    We only ridicule.

And so we lose the things we love,
    When we're not satisfied,
When we make other men into
    What we have fantasized.

So if we take men as they are,
    We'll find each is our friend.
But if we seek to change their ways,
    We'll lose them in the end.

# THE DOMESTICATION OF THE GOAT

The animals all held a belief
  They called reincarnation,
That when they die, they are reborn,
  Another generation.

This creed explains the reason for
  The goat's domestication,
Who took advantage of this belief
  To stop an altercation.

Once from a common water pool
  The animals all drank,
And once each year they all would meet
  To clean their water tank.

And anyone who would not help
  Was sentenced to be killed.
This counteracted selfishness,
  And beasts who were self-willed.

One year the goat did not appear
  To help as others cleaned.
She just had had a baby kid,
  That yet had not been weaned.

# The Domestication of the Goat

A stag was sent to find out why
    The goat had disobeyed,
To ask why she was missing from
    Their annual cleaning day.

She told the stag she'd had a kid.
    He asked, if girl or boy.
Since this stag's mother had just died,
    The goat would pull a ploy.

The goat convinced this trusting stag
    His mother was her kid.
The stag then did the goat no harm,
    In fact, harm he'd forbid.

The antelope then paid a call.
    He asked the young kid's gender.
His father recently had died,
    And wounds of loss were tender.

The goat convinced the antelope
    His father was her kid.
So antelope did goat no harm,
    In fact, harm he'd forbid.

# The Wisdom of African Mythology

So all the different animals
　　Then called upon the goat.
She told them their dead relatives
　　Lived on in her kid's coat.

The leopard was suspicious, though,
　　Of this goat's contradictions.
When in disgust he sprang at her,
　　She fled his jurisdiction.

She ran off then to dwell with men.
　　She's dwelled there ever since.
And leopards still will spring at her,
　　If she escapes her fence.

This proves how lies will complicate
　　The very lives we lead,
For surely we'll be caught in them,
　　And usually with great speed.

If nanny would have told the truth,
　　She would have been believed,
And from her duties cleaning pool,
　　She would have been relieved.

The leopard still would be her pal.
　　All goats could freely roam.
They would not be consigned to pens.
　　The world would be their home.

The liar soon becomes the slave
　　Of stories that he's told.
And things will go from bad to worse,
　　When lies are multifold.

He'll tie himself in endless knots.
　　No one will ever trust him.
He will become the banished fool,
　　For, oh, how lies disgust men.

# WHY HARES HAVE LONG EARS

Yorubas tell a tale about
    Deception in the hare.
It happened when rains ceased to fall,
    And drought was everywhere.

The animals decided that
    They'd cut off tips of ears.
They'd melt them down and sell the fat
    To buy some digging gear.

They'd use this gear to dig a well
    To see them through the drought.
The water they so needed, then,
    Would flow without a doubt.

All animals then snipped their ears,
    As they had promised to,
Except the hare who disappeared
    From everybody's view.

He hid until the waters flowed
    Within their deep, new well.
He then came loudly pounding on
    A calabash and bell.

# Why Hares Have Long Ears

He frightened off the animals,
  Who ran from bell's loud ring.
He drank and bathed within their well,
  As if he were a king.

When other beasts discovered the
  Deception of the hare,
They beat him with their sticks and clubs,
  Until his bones were bare.

He was exiled, but could not hide.
  His ears were just too long.
Both hounds and people searched him out,
  For what he did was wrong.

Those ears the hare refused to cut
  Got him in lots of trouble.
And since each hare has two of them,
  He has his trouble double.

And so the rabbit cannot hide,
  His ears are just too tall.
They stick out high above the grass,
  Just like a target's call.

And men who imitate the hare,
    In cunning and deceit,
Cannot conceal it from their friends
    Whenever they compete.

No man can hide dishonesty.
    It shows upon his face.
Just like the ears of rabbits,
    It points out his disgrace.

# HOW THE TORTOISE GOT REVENGE

The tortoise was in need of salt
   And travelled far to find.
When found, he wrapped it in a bag
   To drag it home behind.

He tugged the string and dragged the salt
   In snail-like transitu.
So patiently he moved along,
   As turtles always do.

Then suddenly the journey stopped.
   A lizard jumped aboard.
He claimed the salt he sat upon,
   Was found and his reward.

The lizard would not be convinced
   The salt was not his find.
And nothing that the turtle said
   Could change the lizard's mind

The tortoise showed he held the string
   That wrapped and pulled the salt.
But greed which blinds one to the truth
   Was lizard's ruling fault.

The tortoise tried explaining things,
    But lizard still insisted,
He found the salt, the salt was his,
    And shouting, he persisted.

The lizard then refused to move,
    'Til elders would decide.
Since they were all his relatives,
    They'd have to take his side.

Each party then explained his case,
    The lizard's case was weak.
But judges who were relatives,
    Sent turtle up a creek.

The lizard argued he had found
    The salt upon the road.
And finders keep, while losers weep,
    As jungle's justice told.

The elders, biased by their kin,
    Said, "Cut the salt in half."
So lizard got one half the salt,
    While turtle got the shaft.

# How the Tortoise Got Revenge

The tortoise sadly left for home.
    His bundle cut in two.
The little salt that he still dragged
    Leaked on the path like dew.

His wife was saddened when she saw,
    What little salt was left.
She knew they were the victims of
    A very clever theft.

The tortoise planned to get revenge,
    By using lizard's trick.
And so with cunning, he set out
    For lizard's bailiwick.

He saw the lizard on the path,
    Stretched out and sound asleep.
Then jumping on the lizard's back,
    The plan he sowed he'd reap.

"Look what I've found upon the road."
    The turtle loudly said.
And as he held the lizard up,
    It wildly shook its head.

"Hey, put me down!" the lizard said,
    And wriggled to get free.
"First, elders must decide our case."
    The turtle said with glee.

The elders were embarrassed by
    This case they had to try.
For fairness meant their past decrees
    Again be verified.

"As we gave judgment for the salt,
    This case demands the same."
"Yes, I agree," the turtle said,
    "And now I stake my claim."

He seized a knife from elder's belt,
    Before the lizard knew,
Then slashed out at the lizard,
    And sliced him right in two.

This was the end of lizard's greed,
    And also of his life.
The turtle lived on happily,
    Both with his salt and wife.

# How the Tortoise Got Revenge

All men who have the curse of greed,
    Are very lizard-like.
They sneak along behind your back,
    Then cowardly they strike.

They cut in two what is not theirs,
    And take the half that's yours.
But justice will at last prevail,
    Experience assures.

Of what they've done to other men
    They each will be accused.
Yes, retribution will win out;
    And wrong will always lose.

I think this has been verified,
    Throughout all history.
But why the greedy will not learn,
    Is nature's mystery.

# THE TORTOISE IS TABOO IN MALAGASY

In seeking food a bird once saw,
    A huge tortoise appear.
He came forth from the sea's great depths,
    To seek a new career.

He said he'd like to know the earth
    And those who lived on land.
The bird said he would be his guide,
    To help him understand.

The tortoise found it hard to walk;
    His feet were just to flat.
They had been made to swim within
    His water habitat.

The bird then made new feet for him,
    Though not a foot physician.
Still those new feet worked very well,
    Like bird was some magician.

They set about exploring things.
    A friendship's tune was sung,
'Til bird plopped on the turtle's shell
    A great big drop of dung.

# The Tortoise is Taboo in Malagasy

"You filthy bird," the turtle cried,
    And caused the bird to flee,
This left the turtle wandering,
    A long way from the sea.

And since that day it's never found
    The sea from which it came.
It slowly walks upon the land,
    And crawls as if it's lame.

Among the Malagasy tribes,
    This turtle's meat's taboo.
For only that which lives on land
    Will that tribe barbecue.

Although this turtle lives on land,
    That's not where it should be.
It should withdraw and realize
    God made it for the sea.

God has a plan for everything,
    Though some don't understand.
They want to stray beyond their bounds,
    Like turtles to dry land.

They want to be what they are not,
    And do what they can't do.
They're never really satisfied,
    With what was hitherto.

The novel has become their god,
    The goal which they pursue.
They brush aside their golden past,
    And only seek what's new.

They simply do not realize,
    Some bird's played them for suckers,
And led them down untraveled roads,
    As if they were lost truckers.

But comes the day of reckoning,
    When all the springs are sprung,
They will discover that they were
    Hit by that dumb bird's dung.

They will cry out and will protest,
    But it will be too late.
As common sense will pass them by
    And leave them to their fate.

# The Tortoise is Taboo in Malagasy

They'll slowly crawl like turtles do
    In searching for the sea.
Still blinded to their golden past,
    Deceived by novelty.

The problem is they never fall
    Upon their face alone.
They seem to hurt the very ones
    They're paid to chaperone.

Perhaps they are just nincompoops,
    Not smart enough to see,
That they should always treasure that
    Which they were born to be.

# THE WHITE MAN COMES TO AFRICA

It seems as though the Africans had an uncanny premonition about the evils which would one day result from the European's invasions of their land. Who else, but the Africans themselves, could have ever known what tragic consequences were impending? Who could have ever guessed the extent or the abuse of the slave trade to the Americas? Who could have possibly realized the terrible evils that would result from a self-indulgent colonialism that would rape a land of its riches in minerals and culture. Somehow the Africans knew?

In Kenya a great witch doctor warned the people he had dreamt strangers would come out of great waters, like yellow frogs with butterfly wings. They would carry sticks that sent out fire (guns) and a great iron snake that spat fire (canon). The witch doctor told them not to fight the strangers when they came, for the strangers would destroy them. The people were told to meet the strangers with courtesy, but never with trust. They were warned never to bring the strangers near their homes or their lands.

King Mugedo of Lovedu prophesied the coming of black ants and red ants. The black ants were the neighboring warlike tribes who would destroy their fellow Africans. The red ants were the Europeans who would exploit them. These two adversaries appeared during the reign of his successors. The black ants were the warring Zulus who were held off by the Lovedu Queen who magically withheld rain to drive them from her land.

King Sobhuza of Swazi dreamed of the coming European invaders as strange people, the color of red porridge, with hair like the tails of cattle. They would come with houses built on platforms pulled by oxen. They would speak barbarian languages and would be ignorant of all human courtesies. They would carry terrible weapons of destruction. He said his dream contained a message from their ancestors not to fight these powerful foreigners, for their weapons made them too powerful to defeat.

Europeans seemed very strange to Africans. They were strange in color, in dress, in language, in manners and courtesies. The Africans knew enough to treat them with caution because of their weapons. Since kindness and hospitality were a part of the ordinary African lifestyle, that same kindness and hospitality was afforded the European visitors. However, the visitors seldom repaid it in kind.

# THE STRANGE STRANGERS

The Europeans were quite strange
    Their color was too pale.
It's too bad, when they landed, though,
    They were not thrown in jail.

The blacks thought whites quite ugly men,
    Whose mothers dressed them funny.
And like all men who live a lie,
    Their mouths twitched like a bunny.

A coward's need invented guns,
    At least in black man's mind.
Who else would strike at enemies,
    From far off or behind?

Whites came with guns against the spear,
    With cannons 'gainst the knife.
They slaughtered all the warriors,
    Then stole the warrior's wife.

They raped the land and stole its gold,
    And robbed it of its culture,
In many ways, whites acted like,
    That bird we call a vulture.

They gave white names to every place,
    As if blacks had no feeling.
They robbed them of their heritage,
    To make their own appealing.

Whites stole from them a treasured past,
    That's never been described.
For when it came to history,
    I'm sure these white men lied.

But slavery was the greatest sin
    Committed by the whites.
To sell a man to servitude
    Denies all human rights.

To rob a land of citizens,
    To steal from it its youth,
Deprives a land of future life
    And all historic truth.

But Africa somehow survived,
    Its trials and tribulations.
Colonialism disappeared,
    With all its aberrations.

And modern states have now sprung up,
    But not in isolation.
They carry scars from past abuse
    And western annexation.

Will these states build on worldliness,
    Acquired from the West?
Or will their ancient heritage
    Be chosen as the best?

# IN CONCLUSION

Yes, be we white, or be we black,
    We each have learned the same.
We blacks have learned past glories.
    We whites have learned past shame.

These myths we've read can teach our world,
    We all have much to learn.
And it will be a wiser world,
    If black myths are not spurned.

All men will find within these myths
    A wisdom and a wit.
And both are needed in this age
    That's chafing at the bit.

All bigotry is ignorance,
    The folly of the fool,
The quackery of idiots,
    Who wasted time in school.

And so all men must now forgive
    Offenses of the past.
And if forgiveness is sincere,
    I'm sure that it will last.

At least it must be tried once more.
   Whites ask another chance.
I know it's asking much of blacks
   To start a fresh romance.

But really there's no other hope,
   For peace among all men.
I know we all have tried it once,
   But we must try again.

And if our efforts are sincere,
   And made with open mind.
Perhaps it won't be long until,
   All men are color-blind.

That is the hope with which I close.
   I hope my faith's well-founded.
And if it is, the future's bright,
   As bright as I've propounded.

# BIBLIOGRAPHY

Abrahams, Roger. African Folktales. New York,
Pantheon Books, 1983.

Abrahamsson, Hans. Origin Of Death: Studies In
African Mythology. New York, Arno Press, 1977.

Ananikian, Mardiros. African Mythology. New York,
Cooper Square, 1964.

Arnott, Kathleen. African Myths and Legends.
New York, H.Z.Walck, 1963.

Brooks, Charlotte. African Rhythms. New York,
Pocket Books, 1974.

Burton, R. Wit And Wisdom From West Africa.
New York, Biblo.

Cardinall, A.W. Tales Told In Togoland.
Oxford, Oxford Press, 1931.

Diop, Cheikh Anta. Precolonial Black Africa.
Brooklyn, Lawrence Hill Books, 1987.

Diop, Cheikh Anta. The African Origin Of
Civilization. New York, Hill, 1974.

Ellis, George. Negro Culture In West Africa.
New York, Neale Publishing Company, 1914.

Feldmann, Susan. African Myths And Tales.
New York, Dell, 1968.

Finnegan, Ruth. Oral Literature In Africa.
Oxford, Oxford Press.

Finnegan, Ruth. Limba Stories And Story Telling.
Oxford, Oxford Press, 1967.

Gates, Henry. The Signifying Monkey. New York,
Oxford Press, 1988.

Gennep, A. The Rite of Passage. London, 1960.

Harris, Joseph, E. Africans And Their History.
New York, New American Library, 1972.

Honey, James. South African Folktales.
New York, Baker-Taylor, 1910.

Hughes, Langston. African Treasury. New York,
Crown Pub., 1960.

Idowu, E.B. Olodumare. London, 1962.

Jones, Edward. Black Zeus; African Mythology.
Seattle, Wash., 1977.

Junod, H.P. Bantu Heritage. Johannesburg, 1938.

Junot, H.A. Life of a South African Tribe. New York,
University Books, 1962

Lee, F.H. Folk Tales of All Nations. New York, Tudor.

Leith-Ross, Sylvia. African Women. New York,
F.A. Praeger, 1965.

Lerer, Susan. African Metalwork and Ivory.
Images of Culture, New Port Beach, CA 92658,1993

Lessing, Doris. African Stories. New York,
Simon and Schuster, 1965.

Lloyd, P.C. Africa In Social Change. London, 1967.

MacCullough, John. The Mythology Of All Races.
(Vol.VII) New York, Cooper Square Pub., 1964.

Mbiti, John. African Religion And Philosophy.
Portsmouth, N.H., Heinemann Press, 1989.

Mitchell, Robert, C., African Primal Religions.
Niles, Ill., Argus, 1977.

Murdock, G.P. Africa: Its People And Their Culture.
New York, 1959.

Okpewho, Isador. Myths In Africa. London,
  Cambridge Press.
Owomoyela, Oyakan. African Literature. Waltham,
  Mass., Crossroads Press, 1979.
Parrinder, E.G. African Traditional Religion.
  New York, Harmondsworth,1969.
Parrinder, E.G. African Mythology. London, Hamlyn,
  1967.
Schebesta, P.I. My Pygmy And Negro Hosts.
  London, E.T., 1936.
Smith, E.W. African Ideas Of God. London, 1961.
Soyinka, W. Myth, Literature, And African World.
  London, Cambridge Press.
Southerland, Rattray. Hausa Folklore, Customs,
  Proverbs. Oxford, Oxford Press, 1913.
Tollerson, Marie. Mythology And Cosmology In The
  Narratives of B. Dadie And B. Diop. Washington,
  Three Continents Press, 1984.
Tanner, R.E. Transition In African Belief.
  Maryknoll, N.Y., 1967.
Tempels, P. Bantu Philosophy. Paris, E.T., 1959.
Van Niekerk, Barand. Negritude In The Work Of
  Leopold Senghor. Cape Town, Balkema 1970.
Werner, A. Myths And Legends Of The Bantu.
  London, 1933.
Woodson, Carter. African Heroes And Heroines.
  Washington, Associated  Publishers, 1969.
Woodson, Carter. African Myths. Washington,
  Associated Pub., 1948.
Young, T.C. African Ways And Wisdom. London, 1937.

# INDEX